VERSES
I
LIKE

SELECTED BY
MAJOR EDWARD BOWES

With a Foreword by
THEODORE ROOSEVELT

GARDEN CITY PUBLISHING COMPANY, INC.
Garden City, New York

TO

MARGARET

ACKNOWLEDGMENTS

THE PUBLISHER has made every effort to trace the owner-
ship of all copyrighted poems. It is his belief that the
necessary permissions from authors or their authorized
agents have been obtained in all cases. In the event of any
question arising as to the use of any poem, the publisher,
while expressing regret for any error he has unconsciously
made, will be pleased to make the necessary correction in
future editions of this book.

Thanks are due to the following authors, publishers,
publications and agents, for permission to use the poems
indicated:

D. Appleton-Century Company—for *To the Fringed Gentian*
from "The Poetical Works of William Cullen Bryant," and
for *Dream Lake* from "The Crimson Tide" by Robert W.
Chambers.

Estate of John Kendrick Bangs—for his poems, *Deliverance,
Blind* and *Gardening*.

Robert Brewster Beattie—for his poem, *A Way to a Happy
New Year*.

Helen K. Bradbury—for Kate Douglas Wiggin's poem, *The Door
Is Open*.

Berton Braley—for his poem, *The Recipe*, which is copyrighted
by him.

Melville Cane and "The New York Herald Tribune"—for his
poem, *Hail to the Major*.

The Citizen, Ottawa, Canada—for the poem, *A Little Rhyme*.

W. B. Conkey Company—for the following poems by Ella
Wheeler Wilcox: *Whatever Is—Is Best, Worth While, Our*

Lives, Life's Scars, The Winds of Fate and *As You Go Through Life*.

Marion Doyle—for her poem, *October*.

Doubleday, Doran & Company, Inc.—for the poem *Gates and Doors* by Joyce Kilmer from "Main Street and Other Poems" by Joyce Kilmer.

Evangelical Publishers, Toronto, Canada—for *What God Hath Promised* by Annie Johnson Flint.

Margaret Fishback and "The New York Herald Tribune"—for her poem *Out of the Woods*.

Spencer Michael Free—for his poem, *The Human Touch*.

Ethel Romig Fuller—for her poem, *Proof* from "Kitchen Sonnets."

Marie Shields Halvey and the Extension Magazine—for her poem *At Parting*.

Harper and Brothers—for *House Blessing* from "The Mirthful Lyre" by Arthur Guiterman.

Dr. M. Coleman Harris—for his poem *A Journey*.

Houghton Mifflin Company—for the following poems: *The Singers, The Heights, The Day Is Done,* and a stanza from *Maidenhood* by Henry Wadsworth Longfellow; *Not What We Give* by James Russell Lowell; *Youth in Our Hearts* by Oliver Wendell Holmes; *A Prayer* from "Lyrics of Joy" by Frank Dempster Sherman.

The International Sunshine Society, Inc.—for *Pass It On* by Henry Burton.

Elsie Janis—for her poem, *My Prayer*.

The Kansas City Star—for the poem, *The Measure of a Man*.

King Features Syndicate, Inc.—for *A Potent Spell* by Aline Michaelis.

Little, Brown and Company—for *Commonplace* from "A Few More Verses" by Susan Coolidge.

Lothrop, Lee and Shepard Company—for *Growing Old* by Marc Eugene Cook.

Douglas Malloch—for his poem, *The Hills Ahead*. Copyright 1926, 1927.

Edwin Markham—for his poems, *A Creed* and *Your Tears*, which are copyrighted by him.

John Martin—for his poem, *These Things Are Free*.

Alice Mattulath—for her poem, *A Pen Portrait of Major Bowes*.

Phyllis McGinley, "The New Yorker" and Harcourt Brace

& Company—for her poem *The Ballad of Amateur Hour* from "One More Manhattan," copyright 1937 by Harcourt Brace.

Meigs Publishing Company—for *Others* by Charles D. Meigs.

The Meredith Publishing Company—for *You Have to Believe* by Douglas Malloch. Copyright 1927.

Madeleine Sweeny Miller—for her poem, *How Far to Bethlehem?*

Martin Panzer—for his poem *October.*

John Oxenham—for his poem, *God's Sunshine.*

The Oxford University Press and Gerald Gurney—for *God's Garden* by Dorothy Frances Gurney.

Edward Hersey Richards—for his poem, *A Wise Old Owl* from "Poems That Reach the Heart."

Winnie Lynch Rockett and The Detroit News—for her poem *His Tender Hands.*

Margaret E. Sangster—for her poems *Tribute, The Blind Man, His Tapestry and Mine,* and *Dedicated to Major Edward Bowes.*

L. Mitchell Thornton—for her poem, *Adventuring.*

Charles Hanson Towne—for his poems, *Needs, Around the Corner, At Nightfall* and *An April Song.*

The Wise Book Company—for *The Value of A Smile* by Wilbur Dick Nesbit.

E. P. Dutton and Company, Inc.—for the following poems by Arthur Guiterman, *To All Friends* from "Song and Laughter" and *House Blessing* from "Death and General Putnam and 101 Other Poems."

Mrs. F. M. Wheeler—for her poem, *The Dollar and the Cent.*

FOREWORD

WE GENERALLY THINK of poetry merely as a means of giving pleasure like a lovely painting. As a matter of fact this is not the case. Of course verse does give pleasure, but that is by no means all that it does. Poetry has shaped history. There is fact, not fiction, in the couplet:

"One man with a dream at pleasure can go out and conquer a crown,
And two with an old song's measure can topple a kingdom down."

King James II was sung out of his kingdom to the verses of

"Lilliburlero bullen a la."

Poetry influences people's lives in marked fashion, and always has done so.

Before printing was invented in the medieval times, bards and minstrels wandered the country. They could be found in the halls of the great castles, in the smoke-filled rooms of the inns, in the market place. They chanted their ballads. Their verses dealt with the heroic deeds of the great heroes and unquestionably inspired many a one to valorous acts.

Not only was there this heroic verse, but also the proverbs, the problems of every-day life were turned into jingles for the average man.

Today verse is just as influential as it ever was, and just as widely read. As Praed said:

> *"I think that life is not too long,*
> *And therefore I determine*
> *That many people read a song*
> *Who will not read a sermon."*

Like the other arts, there are two schools of opinion thereon. One is composed of those people who frankly scorn and dislike the many and pride themselves on appealing only to the few. To them a verse, a bit of prose, a picture, if it carries a general appeal is, *ipso facto,* not art. Of course this is entirely the wrong point of view, for the more general the appeal, the greater the pleasure and the greater the value. There are many couplets which I am willing to admit could not be styled poetry in any strict sense of the word, and yet which to me carry far more appeal than some of the stanzas of far-famed poets.

Major Edward Bowes, who is responsible for this anthology, is a man who believes in the people and who thinks in terms of their problems, sorrows and joys. He has a large sympathy and understanding and that is why at this time he has a greater audience over the air than any other American.

Incidentally, Major Bowes has had a full and varied life of achievement and service. I knew of his record twenty-five years and more ago when I, as a young man, was living in San Francisco.

Those were the days when the city had been shaken by a crusade against vice and corruption. It was one of the first successful crusades conducted in the United States. Prominent among those who initiated it was the foreman of the grand jury, a young fellow called Edward Bowes.

x

He knew everyone and therefore was in a particularly difficult position, for the offenders felt that as he was one of their acquaintances he had no business to prosecute them. Nevertheless, with fine courage, he took the difficult and patriotic course and served decency and the people by taking as his standards for judgment, right and wrong, and nothing else. It is no exaggeration to say that high political honors in California were within his grasp had he cared to go into public life.

At that time he was closely in contact with my father, who had the highest opinion of his character and work. Indeed, their friendship antedates mine. He continued as a friend and admirer of my father throughout my father's life.

Major Bowes' grandfather, the Rev. Adam Ford, was a Methodist preacher in the north of Ireland, and a great influence in his community. He was still active and preaching at eighty-eight, at which age he died. His daughter, Major Bowes' mother, came with her husband to this country. Her husband died when Ed Bowes was only six and left the family practically penniless with three small children of which he was the eldest. Of necessity he became the man of the family. He had to go to work when he graduated from grammar school at the age of thirteen. His education did not stop, however, for his mother (who was a very cultured woman) taught him night after night. The old-fashioned terms and phrases he uses now are due to his close association with her. She was a remarkable woman, for not only did she teach Major Bowes, but his sisters as well, one of whom is a famous pianist and writes verse, some of which is included in this volume.

I think it is because of this background that he is what he is. He touched on life in all its phases and probably that is why his understanding and sympathy are so broad.

His career is an integral part of the great American drama. When he began life he was penniless and unknown. Now there is not a household in the United States where he is a stranger; not only has he given pleasure to millions of listeners, but in addition he has helped them. He has helped them through the quick comprehension and sympathy of which I have spoken, and one of the ways he has done it has been through the verses that he has recited.

Those verses touch a chord. They have been selected by him day by day through his reading. He has picked them not because their authors might be widely known, but because he instinctively felt that they applied to our everyday life and emotions. There is not a verse that he has recited which many persons have not at once felt struck a chord within them. They have ranged from selections from the Bible to chance couplets by anonymous authors.

I know whereof I speak, for I have had different people talk to me of them and ask me if I could recall them, and thereby hangs a tale.

Because of what one man said to me one morning, I went to Major Bowes and told him that I thought he could perform a real service if he would collect the verses he cared for and put them in book form where the average American could have them on his table and refer to them, where they could be a constant and recurring source of pleasure and inspiration.

That is what Major Bowes is doing in this volume, and I am most sincerely happy to have played a part in bringing it into being. I am very happy also to have this chance to write a short foreword not merely for *Verses I Like* collected by Major Bowes, but for the verses for which my friend Ed Bowes cares.

THEODORE ROOSEVELT.

CONTENTS

ANONYMOUS VERSES

xix

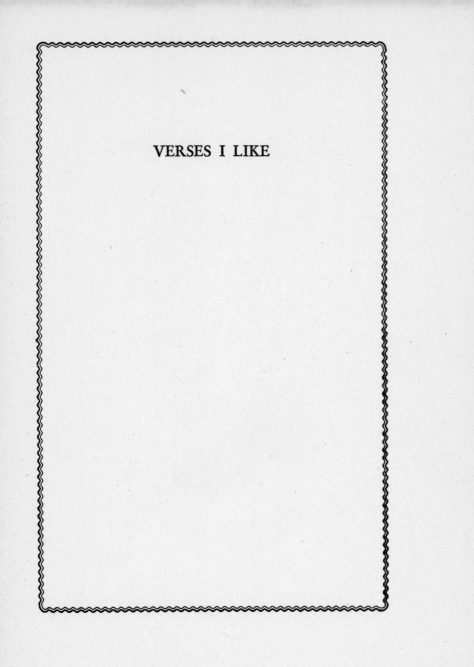

VERSES I LIKE

THERE CAME A MAN

(To Major Edward Bowes on his birthday by his sister)

A MAN did come!
His heart was ever great and kind.
He called to those whose need he knew,
For understanding was his mind.

He called to them to smile and be of cheer,
No longer need they grimly face despair.
The minstrels sallied forth to sing and play,
And leave behind them days of lonely care.

They walked the roads that to their Mecca led,
Or sailed, or rode; alike their hearts were gay;
And there they found that all-protecting arm
Of him whose magic wand can point the way.

The world grows richer now with lovely sound,
Of tender song and chords of sweet allure;
With precious gifts that God alone bestows,
Gifts that might indeed have lain obscure.

Then should we doubt the wisdom of our God,
Who ever does unfold His perfect plan?
He strews His gifts divine on modest brows,
And then in all good time HE SENDS A MAN.

CAROLINE BOWES TOMBO

[23]

WHATEVER IS—IS BEST

I KNOW as my life grows older
And mine eyes have clearer sight—
That under each rank wrong, somewhere
There lies the root of Right!
That each sorrow has its purpose,
By the sorrowing oft unguessed;
But, as sure as the sun brings morning,
Whatever is—is best.

I know that each sinful action,
As sure as the night brings shade,
Is somewhere, sometime punished,
Though the hour be long delayed.
I know that the soul is aided
Sometimes by the heart's unrest,
And to grow means often to suffer—
But whatever is—is best.

I know there are no errors
In the great Eternal plan,
And that all things work together
For the final good of man.
And I know when my soul speeds onward,
In its grand Eternal quest,
I shall say, as I look back earthward,
Whatever is—is best.

ELLA WHEELER WILCOX

THE PATH IN THE SKY

THE woods were dark, and the night was black,
And only an owl could see the track;
But the cheery driver made his way
Through the great pine woods as if it were day.

I asked him, "How do you manage to see?
The road and the forest are one to me."
"To me as well," he replied, "and I
Can only drive by the path in the sky."

I looked above, where the tree tops tall
Rose from the road, like an ebon wall;
And lo! a beautiful starry lane
Wound as the road wound and made it plain.

And since, when the path of my life is drear,
And all is blackness and doubt and fear,
When the horrors of midnight are here below
And I see not a step of the way to go,
Then, ah! then, I can look on high
And walk on earth by the light in the sky.

AMOS R. WELLS

THE HEIGHTS

(From The Ladder of Saint Augustine)

THE heights by great men reached and kept
Were not attained by sudden flight,
But they, while their companions slept
Were toiling upward in the night.
                    HENRY WADSWORTH LONGFELLOW

THE HUMAN TOUCH

'TIS the human touch in this world that counts,
The touch of your hand and mine,
Which means far more to the fainting heart
Than shelter and bread and wine.
For shelter is gone when the night is o'er,
And bread lasts only a day,
But the touch of the hand and the sound of the voice
Sing on in the soul alway.
                    SPENCER MICHAEL FREE

THE GOLDEN SIDE

THERE's many a rest on the road of life,
   If we only would stop to take it;
And many a tone from the better land,
   If the querulous heart would wake it.
To the sunny soul that is full of hope,
   And whose beautiful trust ne'er faileth,
The grass is green and the flowers are bright,
   Though the wintry storm prevaileth.

Better to hope though the clouds hang low,
   And to keep the eyes still lifted;
For the sweet blue sky will soon peep through,
   When the ominous clouds are rifted.
There was never a night without a day,
   Nor an evening without a morning;
And the darkest hour, the proverb goes,
   Is the hour before the dawning.

It's better to weave in the web of life
   A bright and golden filling,
And to do God's will with a ready heart,
   And hands that are swift and willing,
Than to snap the delicate minute threads
   Of our curious lives asunder,
And then Heaven blame for the tangled ends,
   And sit and grieve and wonder.

MARY A. KIDDER

HAPPINESS

"If happiness has not her seat
And center in the breast,
We may be wise, or rich, or great,
But never can be blest."
ROBERT BURNS

NOT WHAT WE GIVE

(*From The Vision of Sir Launfal, Part II*)

NOT what we give, but what we share,
For the gift without the giver is bare;
Who gives himself with his alms feeds three,
Himself, his hungering neighbor, and Me.
JAMES RUSSELL LOWELL

BE THE BEST OF WHATEVER YOU ARE

IF YOU can't be a pine on the top of the hill,
    Be a scrub in the valley—but be
The best little scrub by the side of the rill;
    Be a bush if you can't be a tree.

If you can't be a bush be a bit of the grass,
    And some highway happier make:
If you can't be a muskie, then just be a bass—
    But the liveliest bass in the lake!

We can't all be captains, we've got to be crew,
    There's something for all of us here.
There's big work to do and there's lesser to do,
    And the task we must do is the near.

If you can't be a highway then just be a trail,
    If you can't be the sun, be a star;
It isn't by size that you win or you fail—
    Be the best of whatever you are!
                 DOUGLAS MALLOCH

MEXICAN NIGHT

(Dedicated to Major Edward Bowes, whose voice is heard in many lands, by his sister, Caroline Bowes Tombo)

THE ancient cobbled ways of Ixtopan
Lay warm and quiet neath the setting sun;
Dark heads from casements were withdrawn,
And massive doors closed firmly 'gainst the night
That soon would all enfold until the dawn.

The Plaza, pride of all the town,
Lay glimmering white;
Alone the fountain raised its voice to sing
Sweet tones of sparkling waters
In the fading light.

And all was still.

Then voices, sounding strangely blunt, were heard,
And footsteps ringing loud and strong;
Americanos stalking through the streets
And some Ingles;
And harsher still those Alemans
From on the hill.
All here to bathe in God's warm pools
That heal those who are ill.

They meet, exchange a cheery word, a smile,
Then one by one they follow down a narrow path
In single file.

'Tis Thursday and the hour is eight.
Young Pedro, keeper of the seals of Ixtopan,
Stands waiting at his door, serene, sedate;
His gay serape seeming not one whit too bright
Against his homespun garments snowy white.
The hour tolls from out the tall church tower;
Footsteps quicken—for the host awaits.

With quiet speed the guests are soon in place,
On chairs of garish hue and crude design;
The hand-wrought tapers twinkle flitting smiles,
While modestly the simple folk crowd in,
Their naked feet unheard upon the well-worn tiles.

Before them stands a case of polished wood,
While on the wall of latin blue, above,
There hangs a portrait of the One Who Died,
But rose again to teach us grace and love.

Pedro takes his place with conscious pride.
He turns the dial on the dark-wood box.
When sounds too weird to well define
Scream out at those who wait, intent
To hear the words of one familiar line.

Now Pedro, deft and knowing, yields no ground;
Again the dial moves around.
Aha! 'Tis done! Taut brows are now unbent,
For out upon this mellow Mexican night,
Is launched that welcome voice:

"ALL RIGHT—ALL RIGHT!"

THE RECIPE

It's doing your job the best you can
And being just to your fellow man;
It's making money—but holding friends
And true to your aims and ends;
It's figuring how and learning why
And looking forward and thinking high
And dreaming a little and doing much.
It's keeping always in closest touch
With what is finest in word and deed;
It's being thorough, yet making speed;
It's daring blithely the field of chance
While making labor a brave romance,
It's going onward despite defeat
And fighting staunchly, but keeping sweet;
It's being clean and it's playing fair;
It's laughing lightly at Dame Despair;
It's looking up at the stars above
And drinking deeply of life and love.
It's struggling on with the will to win
But taking loss with a cheerful grin;
It's sharing sorrow and work and mirth
And making better this good old earth;
It's serving, striving through strain and stress;
It's doing your noblest—that's Success!

BERTON BRALEY

HEROISM

THE lives of truest heroism are those in which there are no great deeds to look back upon. It is the little things well done that go to make up a successful and truly good life.

THEODORE ROOSEVELT

YOUTH IN OUR HEARTS

(From Our Indian Summer)

A HEALTH to our future—a sigh for our past,
We love, we remember, we hope to the last;
And for all the base lies that the almanacs hold,
While we've youth in our hearts, we can never grow old!

OLIVER WENDELL HOLMES

WHAT HAVE WE DONE TODAY?

WE SHALL do so much in the years to come,
　But what have we done today?
We shall give our gold in a princely sum,
　But what did we give today?
We shall lift the heart and dry the tear,
We shall plant a hope in the place of fear,
We shall speak the words of love and cheer;
　But what did we speak today?

We shall be so kind in the afterwhile,
　But what have we been today?
We shall bring each lonely life a smile,
　But what have we brought today?
We shall give to truth a grander birth,
And to steadfast faith a deeper worth,
We shall feed the hungering souls of earth;
　But whom have we fed today?

We shall reap such joys in the by-and-by,
　But what have we sown today?
We shall build us mansions in the sky,
　But what have we built today?
'Tis sweet in idle dreams to bask,
But here and now do we do our task?
Yes, this is the thing our souls must ask,
　"What have we done today?"
　　　　　　　　NIXON WATERMAN

BIRTHDAY MESSAGE

(To Major Edward Bowes on his birthday by his sister)

You ask how old am I today,
I know—but I wouldn't care to say;
But if you ask how young I be,
The answer I shall give with glee.
For it is sheer delight to think
That each year ended, forms a link
With one anew—a virgin sheet
That must be filled, as it is meet,
With records of all deeds begun
And ended well, and barring none;
Of days of work, and hours of play,
The weeks a happy roundelay.
The weeks a month, the months a year,
Filled with hope and simple cheer.

To those who see what each year takes,
Who dwell upon the fears and aches
That once have fallen to their lot,
And should indeed be well forgot,
There comes a sorry, creeping age,
A sad, unwanted kind of wage.
But he who looks with cheerful mien,
Whose heart alert, whose spirit keen,
Sees only what the year has brought,
The gain from battles nobly fought.

[35]

So on each birthday start anew,
To pile up gems of precious hue;
Build up a column, beauteous, bright,
That sheds on all a glorious light.

So may you ask how young am I.
I'll tell you that, and even why;
I'm younger today than yesteryear,
More full of hope, less held by fear;
Because I've learned to hold this thought:
That things worth while are dearly bought;
With courage, all can be achieved.
I know. I've worked, I've hoped, and I've believed.

CAROLINE BOWES TOMBO

REAL RICHES

IF INSTEAD of a gem, or even a flower, we could cast the gift of a lovely thought into the heart of a friend, that would be giving as the angels give.

GEORGE MACDONALD

DREAM LAKE

*(Dedicated to Margaret Illington Bowes and
Major Edward Bowes at "Dream Lake")*

I'D RATHER walk with Margaret,
I'd rather talk with Margaret,
And anchor in some sylvan nook
And fish Dream Lake with magic hook
Than sit indoors and write this book.

An author's such an ass, alas!
To watch the world through window glass
When out of doors the skies are fair
And pretty girls beyond compare—
Like Margaret—are strolling there.

I'd rather walk with Edward Bowes,
I'd rather talk with Edward Bowes,
In woodlands where the sunlight gleams
Across the golden Lake of Dreams
Than drive a quill across these reams.

If I could have my proper wish
With these two friends I'd sit and fish
Where sheer cliffs wear their mossy hoods
And Dream Lake widens in the woods,
But Fate says "No! Produce your goods!"

ENVOI

Inspect my goods and choose a few
Dear Margaret, and Edward, too;
Then sink them in the Lake of Dreams
In dim, gold depths where sunshine streams
Down from the sky's unclouded blue,
And I'll be much obliged to you.

ROBERT W. CHAMBERS

UPON LEAVING THE "GOLDEN WEST"!

THE TRAIL

GRAY sage along the "Little Missouri"—
Painted buttes and sapphire sky
The wild wind moans a requiem
And the river sings—"Goodbye."

The ranch house stands lone by the river
And the snow caps gleam in the sun
And the long, long trail far distant winds
Where the fleet footed mustangs run.

There is no round-up by the river now—
No cattle tramp the sage
The rope and the bridle are rotting
And the saddle is green with age.

The strange formations—green and yellow
Gray ghosts—under the moon
At night they join the other shades
With dawn fading all too soon.

Oh! the long, long trail is calling
From the sage 'neath the autumn haze
But I left my shadow to ride the trail
On which I no longer gaze.

MARGARET ILLINGTON BOWES

[38]

GATES AND DOORS
(*A Ballad of Christmas Eve*)

THERE was a gentle hostler
 (And blessed be his name!)
He opened up the stable
 The night Our Lady came.
Our Lady and St. Joseph,
 He gave them food and bed,
And Jesus Christ has given him
 A glory round his head.

So let your gate swing open
 However poor the yard,
Lest weary people visit you
 And find their passage barred.
Unlatch the door at midnight
 And let your lantern's glow
Shine out to guide the traveler's feet
 To you across the snow.

There was a joyous hostler
 Who knelt on Christmas morn
Beside the radiant manger
 Wherein his Lord was born.
His heart was full of laughter,
 His soul was full of bliss,
When Jesus, on His Mother's lap,
 Gave him His hand to kiss.

[39]

Unbar your heart this evening
  And keep no stranger out,
Take from your soul's great portal
  The barrier of doubt.
To humble folk and weary
  Give hearty welcoming,
Your breast shall be to-morrow
  The cradle of a King.

JOYCE KILMER

A LITTLE WORD

A LITTLE word in kindness spoken,
  A motion or a tear,
Has often healed the heart that's broken,
  And made a friend sincere.

A word—a look—has crushed to earth
  Full many a budding flower,
Which, had a smile but owned its birth,
  Would bless life's darkest hour.

Then deem it not an idle thing
  A pleasant word to speak;
The face you wear—the thoughts you bring—
  The heart may heal or break.

DANIEL C. COLESWORTHY

WORTH WHILE

IT IS easy enough to be pleasant
    When life flows by like a song,
But the man worth while is one who will smile
    When everything goes dead wrong.
For the test of the heart is trouble,
    And it always comes with the years,
And the smile that is worth the praises of earth
    Is the one that shines through tears.

It is easy enough to be prudent
    When nothing tempts you to stray,
When without or within no voice of sin
    Is luring your soul away.
But it's only a negative virtue
    Until it is tried by fire,
And the life that is worth the honor of earth
    Is the one that resists desire.

By the cynic, the sad, the fallen,
    Who had no strength for the strife,
The world's highway is cumbered today;
    They make up the item of life.
But the virtue that conquers passion,
    And the sorrow that hides in a smile,—
It is these that are worth the knowledge of earth,
    For we find them but once in a while.

                    ELLA WHEELER WILCOX

LIFE'S MIRROR

THERE are loyal hearts, there are spirits brave,
There are souls that are pure and true,
Then give to the world the best you have,
And the best will come back to you.

Give love, and love to your life will flow,
A strength in your utmost need,
Have faith, and a score of hearts will show
Their faith in your word and deed.

Give truth, and your gift will be paid in kind;
And honor will honor meet;
And a smile that is sweet will surely find
A smile that is just as sweet.

Give pity and sorrow to those who mourn,
You will gather in flowers again
The scattered seeds from your thought out-borne,
Though the sowing seemed but vain.

For life is the mirror of king and slave,
'Tis just what we are and do;
Then give to the world the best you have,
And the best will come back to you.

MADELINE BRIDGES

OUR LIVES

Our lives are songs. God writes the words,
    And we set them to music at pleasure;
And the song grows glad, or sweet, or sad,
    As we choose to fashion the measure.

We must write the music, whatever the song,
    Whatever its rhyme or metre;
And if it is sad, we can make it glad,
    Or, if sweet, we can make it sweeter.

One has a song that is free and strong,
    But the music he writes is minor;
And the sad, sad strain is replete with pain,
    And the singer becomes a repiner.

And he thinks God gave him a dirgelike lay,
    Nor knows that the words are cheery,
And the song seems lonely and solemn—only
    Because the music is dreary.

And the song of another has through the words
    An undercurrent of sadness;
But he sets it to music of ringing chords,
    And makes it a pæan of gladness.

So, whether our songs are sad or not,
    We can give the world more pleasure,
And better ourselves, by setting the words
    To a glad triumphant measure.
                    ELLA WHEELER WILCOX

A LAUGH

A LAUGH is just like sunshine,
    It freshens all the day.
It tips the peaks of life with light
    And drives the clouds away.
The soul grows glad that hears it
    And feels its courage strong;
A laugh is just like sunshine
    For cheering folks along!

A laugh is just like music,
    It lingers in the heart,
And where its melody is heard,
    The ills of life depart;
And happy thoughts come crowding
    Its joyful notes to greet;
A laugh is just like music
    For making living sweet!
                    RIPLEY DUNLAP SAUNDERS

THE SINGERS

GOD sent his Singers upon earth
With songs of sadness and of mirth,
That they might touch the hearts of men,
And bring them back to heaven again.

The first, a youth, with soul of fire,
Held in his hand a golden lyre;
Through groves he wandered, and by streams,
Playing the music of our dreams.

The second, with a bearded face,
Stood singing in the market-place,
And stirred with accents deep and loud
The hearts of all the listening crowd.

A gray old man, the third and last,
Sang in cathedrals dim and vast,
While the majestic organ rolled
Contrition from its mouths of gold.

And those who heard the Singers three
Disputed which the best might be;
For still their music seemed to start
Discordant echoes in each heart.

But the great Master said, "I see
No best in kind, but in degree;
I gave a various gift to each,
To charm, to strengthen, and to teach.

"These are the three great chords of might,
And he whose ear is tuned aright
Will hear no discord in the three,
But the most perfect harmony."
HENRY WADSWORTH LONGFELLOW

A WISE OLD OWL

A WISE old owl sat on an oak,
The more he saw the less he spoke;
The less he spoke the more he heard;
Why aren't we like that wise old bird?
EDWARD HERSEY RICHARDS

THE BLIND MAN

I SEE a blind man every day
Go bravely down the street;
He walks as if the path were clear
Before his steady feet.
Save when he fumbles with his cane,
I almost feel he sees
The passers-by who smile at him,—
The flowers and the trees.

He comes to corners where the crowd
Of traffic swirls about,
But when he hesitates, some hand
Will always help him out.
He crosses pavements fearlessly,—
It is as if he knows
That there are unknown, watchful friends
Along the way he goes!

Sometimes we walk through unseen paths,
Sometimes the road ahead
Is shrouded in the mists of fear;
But we are being led
As surely as the blind man is. . . .
And, if we seem to sway,
A hand will find us in the dark
And guide us on our way.

MARGARET E. SANGSTER

THESE THINGS ARE FREE

IN GLOOMY tones we need not cry,—
"How many things there are to buy!"

Here is a thought for you and me,—
"The best of things in life are free!"

The air, the sunshine and the sea,
All Gladness, beauty,—these are free.

Our faithful friendships, sympathy,
The joys of living,—These are free.

All loving service, loyalty,
Our God's protection.—These are free.

The more we look, the more we see
How many precious things are free.

The heart will find more than the eye
Of things we do not have to buy.

Let's stop and think; let's know and feel
That things like these are truly real,

Yes, think how very rich are we
When all the best of things are free.

                                        JOHN MARTIN

THE VALUE OF A SMILE

THE thing that goes the farthest towards making life
    worth while,
That costs the least and does the most, is just a pleasant
    smile.
The smile that bubbles from a heart that loves its fellow-
    men
Will drive away the cloud of gloom and coax the sun
    again.
It's full of worth and goodness, too, with manly kindness
    blent—
It's worth a million dollars, and it doesn't cost a cent.

There is no room for sadness when we see a cheery smile;
It always has the same good look—it's never out of style—
It nerves us on to try again when failure makes us blue;
The dimples of encouragement are good for me and you,
It pays a higher interest, for it is merely lent—
It's worth a million dollars, and it doesn't cost a cent.

A smile comes very easy—you can wrinkle up with cheer
A hundred times before you can squeeze out a soggy tear.
It ripples out, moreover, to the heart-strings that will tug,
And always leaves an echo that is very like a hug.
So, smile away. Folks understand what by a smile is
    meant—
It's worth a million dollars, and it doesn't cost a cent.

                                    WILBUR DICK NESBIT

DELIVERANCE

I NEVER knew a night so black
Light failed to follow on its track;
I never knew a storm so gray
It failed to have its clearing-day.
I never knew such bleak despair
That there was not a rift, somewhere.
I never knew an hour so drear
Love could not fill it full of cheer!

JOHN KENDRICK BANGS

STANZA

(From The Deserted Village)

WHILE words of learned length and thundering sound
Amazed the gazing rustics ranged around,
And still they gazed, and still the wonder grew,
That one small head could carry all he knew.

OLIVER GOLDSMITH

HAIL TO THE MAJOR

ALL hail to Major Edward Bowes,
Supreme of impresarios,
Who, magically, without theatrics,
Has set a grove around St. Patrick's,
Mightiest feat of legerdemain
Since Birnam moved to Dunsinane.
The ancient stones, austere and papal
He warms with greenery of maple,
Building isles of cloistered shade
For office boy, for man and maid.

But is the major's appetite
For nature satisfied? Not quite.
He looks at John D. junior's realm
Where elm sedately nods to elm,
Then plants his own, to parallel 'm.

And so, municipal thanks we give.
(We hope they'll live, we hope they'll live.)
                              MELVILLE CANE.

THREE GATES

IF YOU are tempted to reveal
A tale some one to you has told
About another, make it pass,
Before you speak, three gates of gold.

These narrow gates: First—"Is it true?"
Then "Is it needful?" In your mind
Give truthful answer. And the next
Is last and narrowest—"Is it kind?"

And if to reach your lips at last
It passes through these gateways three,
Then you may tell the tale, nor fear
What the result of speech may be.

                                    BETH DAY

WHAT I LIVE FOR

I LIVE for those who love me,
　For those I know are true,
For the heaven that smiles above me,
　And awaits my spirit, too;
For the human ties that bind me,
For the tasks by God assigned me,
For the bright hopes left behind me,
　And the good that I can do.

I live to learn their story
　Who've suffered for my sake,
To emulate their glory,
　And follow in their wake;
Bards, martyrs, patriots, sages,
The noble of all ages,
Whose deeds crown hist'ry's pages,
　And Time's great volume make.

I live to hail the season,
　By gifted minds foretold,
When men shall rule by reason,
　And not alone by gold—
When man to man united,
And every wrong thing righted,
The whole world shall be lighted
　As Eden was of old.

[53]

I live to hold communion
  With all that is divine,
To feel there is a union
  'Twixt Nature's heart and mine;
To profit by affliction,
Reap truths from fields of fiction,
Grow wiser from conviction,
  And fulfill each grand design.

I live for those who love me,
  For those who know me true,
For the heaven that smiles above me,
  And awaits my spirit, too;
For the wrong that needs resistance,
For the cause that lacks assistance,
For the future in the distance,
  And the good that I can do.
GEORGE LINNAEUS BANKS

UNIVERSAL LANGUAGE

IN EVERY race, in every creed,
It matters not how far apart,
The language of a loving deed
Is understood by every heart.
JOSEPHINE ROBINSON

HOW LITTLE IT COSTS

How little it costs, if we give it a thought,
  To make happy some heart each day!
Just one kind word, or a tender smile,
  As we go on our daily way.
Perchance a look will suffice to clear
  The cloud from a neighbor's face,
And the press of a hand in sympathy
  A sorrowful tear efface.

One walks in sunlight, another goes
  All wearily in the shade;
One treads a path that is fair and smooth,
  Another must pray for aid.
O'er ways that are rough with stumbling stones,
  Where the tired feet go slow,
One sees with eyes which are glad and bright,
  Another's with tears o'erflow.

We pass each other as days go by,
  But we seldom have time to heed—
We who are filled with our own content—
  How much our neighbors may need.
Can't we stop to give just a kindly smile?
  Or a tender word or so?
Or only one glance of sympathy
  Which might to some sad heart go?

[55]

And kindle therein a glow of trust,
  And dry the falling tears,
And help sweet faith to revive again
  In the place of grief and fears?
It costs so little! I wonder why
  We give it so little thought!
A smile—kind words—a glance—a touch!
  What magic with them is wrought!

MARY DOW BRINE

A CREED

THERE is a destiny that makes us brothers:
  None goes his way alone:
All that we send into the lives of others
  Comes back into our own.

I care not what his temples or his creeds,
  One thing holds firm and fast—
That into his fateful heap of days and deeds
  The soul of a man is cast.

EDWIN MARKHAM

THEY DO NOT KNOW

THEY do not know the harm they do,
  Who say an unkind thing;
The hasty word, by them forgot,
  In some heart leaves a sting.

They never know the ill they do
  By some unfriendly deed;
Or what a harvesting of tares
  Where they have sown the seed!

They do not know the good they do,
  Who speak a heartening phrase,
Or lend a helping hand along
  Life's steep and rugged ways.

They never know the good they do,
  Who cheer, and laugh, and sing,
And so into a toil-filled day,
  A happier courage bring.

O careless ones, think what you do;
  Take heed to what you say;
And, kindly ones, speak, laugh, and sing,
  And cheer us on our way!

EMMA A. LENT

NOBLESSE OBLIGE

If I am weak and you are strong,
  Why then, why then,
To you the braver deeds belong;
  And so, again,
If you have gifts and I have none,
If I have shade and you have sun,
'Tis yours with freer hand to give,
'Tis yours with truer grace to live,
Than I, who giftless, sunless, stand
With barren life and hand.

'Tis wisdom's law, the perfect code,
  By love inspired;
Of him on whom much is bestowed
  Is much required.
The tuneful throat is bid to sing,
The oak must reign the forest's king;
The rustling stream the wheel must move,
The beaten steel its strength must prove.
'Tis given unto the eagle's eyes
To face the midday skies.

CARLOTTA PERRY

A POTENT SPELL

A LITTLE hope, a little cheer
　　To bless the busy day;
Ah, what a potent spell is here
　　To charm dark fears away!

As swiftly as the passing wind,
　　So runs time's caravan,
Then why not labor to be kind
　　In every way we can?

The chance is with us every hour
　　To do some deed of good,
To make life's desert places flower
　　With some blithe-hearted mood.

A little smile, a little trust,
　　A little word of faith
Can dim harsh memories unjust
　　And sorrow's wistful wraith.

As swiftly as the passing wind,
　　So runs time's caravan,
And ah! the joy of being kind,
　　Always, to every man!
　　　　　　　ALINE MICHAELIS

THE LAW OF LOVE

MAKE channels for the streams of love
   Where they may broadly run,
And love has overflowing streams
   To fill them every one.

For we must share if we would keep
   That blessing from above;
Ceasing to give, we cease to have,—
   Such is the law of love.
                  RICHARD CHEVENIX TRENCH

THE PERFECT LIGHT

THERE is a light beyond the light
   That shines in human eyes;
'Tis not the light of moon or stars
   Or of the bright sunrise.
It is the lovelight in your heart
   And if you're filled with grace
This perfect light of perfect love
   Will shine out in your face.
                  G. W. GAGE

LIFE'S SCARS

THEY say the world is round, and yet
   I often think it square,
So many little hurts we get
   From corners here and there.
But one great truth in life I've found,
   While journeying to the West,
The only folks who really wound
   Are those we love the best.

The man you thoroughly despise
   Can rouse your wrath, 'tis true;
Annoyance in your heart will rise
   At things mere strangers do;
But those are only passing ills,
   This rule all lives will prove:
The rankling wound which aches and thrills
   Is dealt by hands we love.

The choicest garb, the sweetest grace,
   Are oft to strangers shown;
The careless mien, the frowning face,
   Are given to our own.
We flatter those we scarcely know,
   We please the fleeting guest,
And deal full many a thoughtless blow
   To those who love us best.

Love does not grow on every tree,
   Nor true hearts yearly bloom.
Alas, for those who only see
   This cut across a tomb!
But, soon or late, the fact grows plain
   To all through sorrow's test;
The only folks who give us pain
   Are those we love the best.
             ELLA WHEELER WILCOX

COURTESY

How sweet and gracious, even in common speech,
Is that fine sense which men call Courtesy!
Wholesome as air and genial as the light,
Welcome in every clime as breath of flowers,—
It transmutes aliens into trusting friends,
And gives its owner passport round the globe.
             JAMES T. FIELDS

THE HILLS AHEAD

The hills ahead look hard and steep and high,
And often we behold them with a sigh;
But as we near them level grows the road,
We find on every slope, with every load,
The climb is not so steep, the top so far,
The hills ahead look harder than they are.

And so it is with troubles, though they seem so great
That men complain and fear and hesitate,
Less difficult the journey than we dreamed,
It never proves as hard as once it seemed;
There never comes a hill, a task, a day,
But as we near it, easier the way.

Douglas Malloch

THE WINDS OF FATE

One ship drives east and another drives west
With the selfsame winds that blow.
'Tis the set of the sails
And not the gales
Which tells us the way to go.

[63]

Like the winds of the sea are the ways of fate;
As we voyage along through life,
'Tis the set of a soul
That decides its goal,
And not the calm or the strife.
ELLA WHEELER WILCOX

IMITATION OF HORACE

(Book III, Ode 29)

HAPPY the man, and happy he alone,
He who can call today his own;
He who, secure within, can say,
Tomorrow, do thy worst, for I have lived today.
Be it fair, or foul, or rain, or shine,
The joys I have possessed in spite of fate, are mine;
Not heaven itself upon the past has power;
But what has been, has been, and I have had my hour.
JOHN DRYDEN

GOD'S SUNSHINE

NEVER once since the world began
Has the sun ever stopped shining.
His face very often we could not see,
And we grumbled at his inconstancy;
But the clouds were really to blame, not he,
For, behind them, he was shining.

And so, behind life's darkest clouds,
God's love is always shining.
We veil it at times with our faithless fears,
And darken our sight with our foolish tears,
But in time the atmosphere always clears,
For His love is always shining.

JOHN OXENHAM

STARS IN DARKNESS

DARKNESS makes us aware of the stars,
And so when dark hours arise,
They may hold a bright and lovely thing,
We might never have known otherwise.

PETER A. LEA

[65]

AS YOU GO THROUGH LIFE

DON'T look for the flaws as you go through life;
    And even when you find them,
It is wise and kind to be somewhat blind
    And look for the virtue behind them,
For the cloudiest night has a hint of light
    Somewhere in its shadows hiding,
It is better by far to hunt for a star
    Than the spots on the sun abiding.

The current of life runs ever away
    To the bosom of God's great ocean.
Don't set your force 'gainst the river's course
    And think to alter its motion.
Don't waste a curse on the universe—
    Remember it lived before you.
Don't butt at the storm with your puny form,
    But bend and let it go o'er you.

This world will never adjust itself
    To suit your whims to the letter;
Some things must go wrong your whole life long,
    And the sooner you know it the better.
It is folly to fight with the Infinite,
    And go under at last in the wrestle,
The wiser man shapes into God's plan
    As the water shapes into a vessel.

ELLA WHEELER WILCOX

DEDICATED TO
MAJOR EDWARD BOWES

SOMEWHERE a blessed garden grows,
  With rosemary and rue—
And in among the flowers, we find
  Frail dreams that have come true.
We find the whisper of a prayer,
  The ghost of vanished youth—
The love that we have lost awhile,
  The warm perfume of truth.

Somewhere a blessed garden grows,
  And when the way seems hard,
If we can catch a glimpse of it,
  We feel new faith in God.
For, oh, it is in certain hearts
  That this rare beauty glows;
I always find my garden spot,
  When I'm with Major Bowes!
                MARGARET E. SANGSTER

GOOD-NIGHT

SLEEP sweetly in this quiet room,
   O thou, whoe'er thou art,
And let no mournful yesterday
   Disturb thy quiet heart.

Nor till tomorrow mar thy rest
   With dreams of coming ill,
Thy Maker is thy changeless friend,
   His love surrounds thee still.

Forget thyself and all the world,
   Put out each feverish light,
The stars are watching overhead,
   Sleep sweetly then, good-night.
   ELLEN M. HUNTINGTON GATES

PRAYER

GOD, give me sympathy and sense,
And help to keep my courage high;
God, give me calm and confidence,
And—please—a twinkle in my eye.
   MARGARET BAILEY

AT PARTING

In every land the language knows
   Some tender, singing word
That always, when the parting guest
   Speeds on his way, is heard.

With "Au revoir," "Auf wiedersehn,"
   "Adios" or "Farewell,"
Each meant, for sweet remembrance sake
   The heart's good wish to tell.

But I like best the Mexican
   That holds all needs of men:
"God keep you, friend, in grace and health
   Until we meet again."
                MARIE SHIELDS HALVEY

NEEDS

I WANT a little house
Upon a little hill,
With lilacs laughing at the door
When afternoons are still.

I want an apple tree
Laden with drifts of bloom;
I want blue china all about
In every little room.

I want a little path
Bordered with brilliant phlox,
And on each window sill I want
A painted flower box.

And then—I want you there
In sun, and frost, and rain,
To smile when I come trudging home
Through a dim, scented lane.

For what's a little house
Upon a little hill,
Unless you light the fire for me
When nights are strangely still?

CHARLES HANSON TOWNE

ADVENTURING

I WANT to go far, far away
    Into a distant land,
But darkest night would be each day
    Unless I held your hand.

I want to see a people new,
    Some unknown race my choice,
But I should wish my journey through
    Unless I heard your voice.

I want adventuring to go,
    Bold deeds I'd like to do.
But, deep within my heart I know,
    I'd rather stay with you.
        L. MITCHELL THORNTON

THE LITTLE RIFT

(From Idylls of the King: Merlin and Vivien)

IT IS the little rift within the lute,
That by and by will make the music mute,
And ever widening slowly silence all.
        ALFRED TENNYSON

AROUND THE CORNER

AROUND the corner I have a friend,
In this great city that has no end;
Yet days go by, and weeks rush on,
And before I know it a year is gone,
And I never see my old friend's face,
For Life is a swift and terrible race.
He knows I like him just as well
As in the days when I rang his bell
And he rang mine. We were younger then,
And now we are busy, tired men:
Tired with playing a foolish game,
Tired with trying to make a name.
"To-morrow," I say, "I will call on Jim,
Just to show that I'm thinking of him."
But to-morrow comes—and to-morrow goes,
And the distance between us grows and grows.

Around the corner!—yet miles away. . . .
"Here's a telegram, sir. . . ."
                    "Jim died to-day."
And that's what we get, and deserve in the end:
Around the corner, a vanished friend.
                    CHARLES HANSON TOWNE

HIS TENDER HANDS

His tender hands have fashioned tiny Things:
The wee blue petals of forget-me-nots;
A drop of mist; an insect's tissue wings:
A poppy seed; a caterpillar's spots;
The sensitive antennae of a bee;
Each amber globule of the desert sands—
Then shall I fear, when He has said to me,
"Thy days, my little one, are in my hands?"

WINNIE LYNCH ROCKETT

A CHILD'S PRAYER

(Favorite of Mrs. Edith Kermit Roosevelt)

"MAKE ME, dear Lord, polite and kind,
To every one, I pray.
And may I ask you how you find
Yourself, dear Lord, today?"

JOHN BANNISTER TABB

MY PRAYER

GOD, let me live each lovely day
So I may know that, come what may,
I've done my best to live the way
　　You'd want me to.

Just let me know, if I should stray,
That I may stop along the way
At any time of night or day
　　And talk to You.

ELSIE JANIS (1921)

TOO LATE

WHAT silences we keep, year after year
With those who are most near to us, and dear!
We live beside each other day by day,
And speak of myriad things, but seldom say
The full, sweet word that lies within our reach
Beneath the common ground of common speech.

Then out of sight and out of reach they go—
These close, familiar friends who loved us so;
And, sitting in the shadow they have left,
Alone with loneliness, and sore bereft,
We think with vain regret of some fond word
That once we might have said and they have heard.

For weak and poor, the love that we expressed
Now seems beside the vast, sweet unexpressed,
And slight the deeds we did, to those undone,
And small the service spent, to treasure won,
And undeserved the praise for word and deed
That should have overflowed the simple need.

This is the cruel cross of life,—to be
Full visioned only when the ministry
Of death has been fulfilled, and in the place
Of some dear presence is but empty space.
What recollected services can then
Give consolation for the "might have been"?

NORA PERRY

A PRAYER

It is my joy in life to find
At every turning of the road,
The strong arm of a comrade kind
To help me onward with my load.

And since I have no gold to give,
And love alone must make amends,
My only prayer is, while I live,—
God make me worthy of my friends!
FRANK DEMPSTER SHERMAN

YOUR TEARS

I dare not ask your very all,
    I only ask a part;
Bring me, when dancers leave the hall,
    Your aching heart.
Give other friends your lighted face,
    The laughter of the years;
I come to crave a greater grace—
    Bring me your tears.
EDWIN MARKHAM

[76]

LIGHT

THE night has a thousand eyes,
    And the day but one;
Yet the light of the bright world dies
    With the dying sun.

The mind has a thousand eyes,
    And the heart but one;
Yet the light of a whole life dies,
    When love is done.
        FRANCIS WILLIAM BOURDILLON

AT NIGHTFALL

I NEED so much the quiet of your love
    After the day's loud strife;
I need your calm all other things above
    After the stress of life.

I crave the haven that in your dear heart lies
    After all toil is done;
I need the star-shine of your heavenly eyes
    After the day's great sun!
        CHARLES HANSON TOWNE

TO KNOW ALL IS TO FORGIVE ALL

IF I knew you and you knew me,—
If both of us could clearly see,
And with an inner sight divine
The meaning of your heart and mine,
I'm sure that we would differ less
And clasp our hands in friendliness;
Our thoughts would pleasantly agree
If I knew you and you knew me.

If I knew you and you knew me,
As each one knows his own self, we
Would look each other in the face
And see therein a truer grace.
Life has so many hidden woes,
So many thorns for every rose;
The "why" of things our hearts would see,
If I knew you and you knew me.

NIXON WATERMAN

OCTOBER

OCTOBER, October,
The word is like a song
  Of drowsy dreams
  And lilting themes
That creep and sweep along.

October, October,
Within your singing name
  Are mornings bright
  With amber light,
With blue and purple flame.

October, October,
A dancing gypsy girl,
  Whose scarf is pinned
  To a rainbow wind
And blown across the world.
MARION DOYLE

*   *   *

OCTOBER is a lovely month,
My sisters and my brothers;
October is a lovely month—
And so are all the others!
MARTIN PANZER

[79]

WHAT GOD HATH PROMISED

God hath not promised
Skies always blue,
Flower-strewn pathways
All our lives through;
God hath not promised
Sun without rain,
Joy without sorrow,
Peace without pain.

But God hath promised
Strength for the day,
Rest for the labor,
Light for the way,
Grace for the trials,
Help from above,
Unfailing sympathy,
Undying love.

ANNIE JOHNSON FLINT

THERE'S A WIDENESS IN GOD'S MERCY

THERE's a wideness in God's mercy,
　　Like the wideness of the sea;
There's a kindness in His justice,
　　Which is more than liberty. . . .

For the love of God is broader
　　Than the measure of man's mind;
And the heart of the Eternal
　　Is most wonderfully kind.

If our love were but more simple,
　　We should take Him at His word,
And our lives would be all sunshine
　　In the sweetness of our Lord.
　　　　　　FREDERICK W. FABER

THE TWENTY–THIRD PSALM

(David's Confidence in God's Grace)

THE Lord is my shepherd,
I shall not want.

He maketh me to lie down
in green pastures; he leadeth me beside
the still waters.

He restoreth my soul; he
leadeth me in the paths of righteousness
for his name's sake.

Yea, though I walk through
the valley of the shadow of death, I
will fear no evil; for thou art with me;
thy rod and thy staff they comfort me.

Thou preparest a table before
me in the presence of mine enemies; thou
anointest my head with oil; my cup runneth
over.

Surely goodness and mercy
shall follow me all the days of my life;
and I will dwell in the house of the Lord
for ever.

PASS IT ON

HAVE you had a kindness shown?
  Pass it on.
'Twas not given for thee alone,
  Pass it on.
Let it travel down the years,
Let it wipe another's tears,
Till in heav'n the deed appears—
  Pass it on.

Did you hear the loving word?
  Pass it on—
Like the singing of a bird?
  Pass it on.
Let its music live and grow,
Let it cheer another's woe;
You have reaped what others sow—
  Pass it on.

'Twas the sunshine of a smile—
  Pass it on.
Staying but a little while!
  Pass it on.
April beam a little thing,
Still it wakes the flowers of spring,
Makes the silent birds to sing—
  Pass it on.

Have you found the heavenly light?
   Pass it on.
Souls are groping in the night,
   Daylight gone—
Hold thy lighted lamp on high,
Be a star in someone's sky,
He may live who else would die—
   Pass it on.

Be not selfish in thy greed,
   Pass it on.
Look upon thy brother's need,
   Pass it on.
Live for self, you live in vain;
Live for Christ, you live again;
Live for Him, with Him you reign—
   Pass it on.

HENRY BURTON

LEAD, KINDLY LIGHT

LEAD, kindly Light, amid the encircling gloom,
　　　　Lead Thou me on!
The night is dark, and I am far from home—
　　　　Lead Thou me on!
Keep Thou my feet; I do not ask to see
The distant scene,—one step enough for me.

I was not ever thus, nor prayed that Thou
　　　　Shouldst lead me on.
I loved to choose and see my path; but now
　　　　Lead Thou me on!
I loved the garish day, and, spite of fears,
Pride ruled my will: remember not past years.

So long Thy power hath blest me, sure it still
　　　　Will lead me on,
O'er moor and fen, o'er crag and torrent, till
　　　　The night is gone;
And with the morn those angel faces smile
Which I have loved long since, and lost awhile.
　　　　JOHN HENRY, CARDINAL NEWMAN

EN VOYAGE

WHICHEVER way the wind doth blow,
Some heart is glad to have it so;
Then, blow it east, or blow it west,
The wind that blows, that wind is best.

My little craft sails not alone;
A thousand fleets from every zone
Are out upon a thousand seas;
What blows for one a favoring breeze
Might dash another with the shock
Of doom upon some hidden rock.

And so I do not dare to pray
For winds to waft me on my way,
But leave it to a higher Will
To stay or speed me, trusting still
That all is well, and sure that He
Who launched my bark will sail with me
Through storm and calm, and will not fail,
Whatever breezes may prevail,
To land me, every peril past,
Within the sheltered haven at last.

Then, whatsoever wind doth blow,
My heart is glad to have it so;
And, blow it east, or blow it west,
The wind that blows, that wind is best.

CAROLINE ATHERTON MASON

[86]

NOW

THE clock of life is wound but once,
  And no man has the power
To tell just when the hands will stop—
  At late or early hour.
Now is the only time you own:
  Live, love, work with a will.
Place no faith in tomorrow, for—
  The clock may then be still.

GEORGE H. CANDLER

GROW OLD ALONG WITH ME

(*From Rabbi Ben Ezra*)

GROW old along with me!
The best is yet to be,
The last of life, for which the first was made:
Our times are in His hand
Who saith, "A whole I planned,
Youth shows but half; trust God: see all, nor be afraid!"

ROBERT BROWNING

[87]

BLIND

"Show me your God!" the doubter cries.
I point him to the smiling skies;
I show him all the woodland greens;
I show him peaceful sylvan scenes;
I show him winter snows and frost;
I show him waters tempest-tossed;
I show him hills rock-ribbed and strong;
I bid him hear the thrush's song;
I show him flowers in the close—
The lily, violet and rose;
I show him rivers, babbling streams;
I show him youthful hopes and dreams;
I show him maids with eager hearts;
I show him toilers in the marts;
I show him stars, the moon, the sun;
I show him deeds of kindness done;
I show him joy, I show him care,
And still he holds his doubting air,
And faithless goes his way, for he
Is blind of soul, and cannot see!

JOHN KENDRICK BANGS

WISER TODAY

(From Thoughts On Various Subjects)

A MAN should never be ashamed
to say he has been in the wrong, which
is but saying in other words that he is
wiser today than he was yesterday.
                                    ALEXANDER POPE

STUMBLING–BLOCK OR STEPPING–STONE

ISN'T it strange that princes and kings
And clowns that caper in sawdust rings
And common folks like you and me
     Are builders of eternity?
To each is given a bag of tools,—
A shapeless mass and a book of rules;
And each must make, ere life is flown,
A stumbling-block or a stepping-stone.
                                    R. L. SHARPE

A PEN PORTRAIT OF MAJOR BOWES

An Acrostic

Each Sunday morn his kindly voice we hear,
Doing his bit to bring to others cheer
Who need a friendly word, uplifting thought
And lovely music to their fireside brought.
Real joy he finds when those whose hearts were sore,—
Dejected ones, the aged, ailing, lone,—
Because of what he says, now grieve no more,
Or have, through what he gives, some comfort known;
When hungry souls with beauty he can feed,
Enriching all and planting useful seed:
Such is the man whom old and young hold dear!

ALICE MATTULATH

COMMONPLACE

A COMMONPLACE life we say, and we sigh;
    But why should we sigh as we say?
The commonplace sun in the commonplace sky
    Makes up the commonplace day.
The moon and the stars are commonplace things,—
The flower that blooms and the bird that sings;
    But sad were the world and dark our lot
If the flowers failed and the sun shone not;—
    And God, who sees each separate soul,
Out of commonplace lives makes His beautiful whole.
                    SUSAN COOLIDGE

PROOF

IF RADIO's slim fingers can pluck a melody
From night—and toss it over a continent or sea;
If the petaled white notes of a violin
Are blown across the mountains or the city's din;
If songs, like crimson roses, are culled from thin blue air—
Why should mortals wonder if God hears prayer?
                  ETHEL ROMIG FULLER

"OTHERS"

LORD, help me live from day to day
In such a self-forgetful way
That even when I kneel to pray,
My prayer shall be for—Others.

Help me in all the work I do
To ever be sincere and true
And know that all I'd do for you,
Must needs be done for—Others.

Let "Self" be crucified and slain,
And buried deep; and all in vain
May efforts be to rise again,
Unless to live for—Others.

And when my work on earth is done,
And my new work in Heaven's begun,
May I forget the crown I've won,
While thinking still of—Others.

Others, Lord, yes, others.
Let this my motto be,
Help me to live for others,
That I may live like Thee.

CHARLES D. MEIGS

A DREAM REALIZED

SOMETIMES God bids us take a step,
  Sometimes He bids us stay,
But whether it be go or wait,
  He leads us every day.

For many years our thoughts have turned
  Toward some expansion plan,
But never could we see the goal
  As well as now we can.

The way is clear, the privilege ours,
  Let naught retard the thrill
That comes with leading souls to do
  Our blessed Master's will.
                    JESSE L. BERNHEISEL

BALLAD OF AMATEUR HOUR

WHAT shall we do with the bold milkman
    Who loud in the little hours
Whistles away like a hearty Pan
    Till slumber deserts our bowers?

He shall whistle an air for Major Bowes,
    The best that his tongue can twist to;
And a thousand milkmen will vote him first
And night after night will his lips be pursed
In the very tune that we called accursed,
    For a suffering world to list to.

What shall we do with the grocer's boy
    Whose resonant warblings fret us,
As he chants to the cheeses for simple joy
    Or lyrically wraps the lettuce?

Why, he shall warble for Major Bowes,
    Later, my friends, or sooner.
And never, ah never again will he
Sing to the squash and the broccoli,
But now in radio ranks shall be
    Numbered another crooner.

What shall we do with the neighbors' brood
　Who, shrill and fierce as hornets,
Shatter the spell of our solitude
　With fiddles and fifes and cornets?

Why, they shall serenade Major Bowes
　With cornet and fife and fiddle.
Such sound and fury they'll all display
That the tones which frightened the Muse away
We shall hear by night, we shall hear by day,
　Whenever a dial we twiddle.

What shall we do with the family bore
　Whose persiflage never ceases?
And what with the audible miss next door
　Who's clever at speaking pieces?

Why, they shall babble for Major Bowes
　Their artful impersonations.
And an affable agent will bid them sign
A contract, square on the dotted line,
For alternate evenings at half-past nine
　On very distinguished stations.

What shall we do with Major Bowes,
　Lord of the aerial garden,
Who turns our amateurs into pros
　With never a Beg Your Pardon?

When the world is so full of a number of sounds,
  When the air repents its store
Of tenors and torchers and boop-a-doopers,
Of Kiddie Koncerts and Drama Groupers,
Of yodellers yodelling cowboy ballads,
Of commentators on books and salads,
Of those who imitate birds and breezes,
Of bearded jests and of ancient wheezes,
What shall we do with the man who'd seek
Sunday by Sunday and week by week
  To swell the flood with more?

What shall we do with Major Bowes?
Nobody knows, nobody knows.

PHYLLIS McGINLEY

HOW FAR TO BETHLEHEM?

"How far is it to Bethlehem town?"
Just over Jerusalem hills adown,
Past lovely Rachel's white-domed tomb—
Sweet shrine of motherhood's young doom.

It isn't far to Bethlehem town—
Just over the dusty roads adown,
Past Wise Men's well, still offering
Cool draughts from welcome wayside spring;
Past shepherds with their flutes of reed
That charm the woolly sheep they lead;
Past boys with kites on hilltops flying,
And soon you're there where Bethlehem's lying.
Sunned white and sweet on olived slopes,
Gold-lighted still with Judah's hopes.

And so we find the Shepherd's field
And plain that gave rich Boaz yield;
And look where Herod's villa stood.
We thrill that earthly parenthood
Could foster Christ who was all-good;
And thrill that Bethlehem town to-day
Looks down on Christian homes that pray.

It isn't far to Bethlehem town!
It's anywhere that Christ comes down
And finds in people's friendly face
A welcome and abiding place.
The road to Bethlehem runs right through
The homes of folks like me and you.
MADELEINE SWEENY MILLER

HOUSE BLESSING

BLESS the four corners of this house,
    And be the lintel blest;
And bless the hearth and bless the board
    And bless each place of rest;
And bless the door that opens wide
    To stranger as to kin;
And bless each crystal window-pane
    That lets the starlight in;
And bless the rooftree overhead
    And every sturdy wall.
The peace of man, the peace of God,
    The peace of Love on all!
ARTHUR GUITERMAN

CHRISTMAS CAROL

THE earth has grown old with its burden of care,
   But at Christmas it always is young,
The heart of the jewel burns lustrous and fair,
And its soul full of music breaks forth on the air,
   When the song of the angels is sung.

It is coming, Old Earth, it is coming to-night!
   On the snowflakes which cover thy sod,
The feet of the Christ-child fall gentle and white,
And the voice of the Christ-child tells out with delight,
   That mankind are the children of God.

On the sad and the lonely, the wretched and poor,
   That voice of the Christ-child shall fall,
And to every blind wanderer opens the door
Of a hope that he dared not to dream of before,
   With a sunshine of welcome for all.

The feet of the humblest may walk in the field
   Where the feet of the Holiest have trod.
This, this is the marvel to mortals revealed
When the silvery trumpets of Christmas have pealed,
   That mankind are the children of God.

PHILLIPS BROOKS

TRUE REST

Rest is not quitting
The busy career;
Rest is the fitting
Of self to one's sphere.

'Tis the brook's motion,
Clear without strife,
Fleeting to ocean,
After this life.

'Tis loving and serving,
The highest and best;
'Tis onward, unswerving,
And this is true rest.
JOHANN WOLFGANG GOETHE

LIFE'S COMMON THINGS

THE things of every day are all so sweet—
The morning meadows wet with dew,
The dance of daisies in the noon; the blue
Of far-off hills where twilight shadows lie;
The night, with all its tender mystery of sound
And silence, and God's starry sky;
Oh, life—the whole of life—is far too fleet,
The things of every day are all so sweet.

The common things of life are all so dear—
The waking in the warm half gloom
To find again the old familiar room,
The scents and sights and sounds that never tire;
The homely work, the plans, the lilt of baby's laugh,
The crackle of the open fire;
The waiting, then the footsteps coming near,
The opening door, your hand-clasp, and your kiss—
Is Heaven not after all the Now and Here?
The common things of life are all so dear.

ALICE E. ALLEN

OUT OF THE WOODS

LET us extend to Major Bowes
A laurel wreath, a palm, a rose;
A metropolitan citation
For his superlative donation
To Gotham. All those maple trees
He's planting at St. Patrick's please
Us godless city dwellers so
They're putting us in mind to go
Back to the churches whence we sprung
When we were reverent and young.
                        MARGARET FISHBACK

HOUSE AND HOME

A HOUSE is built of bricks and stones, of sills and posts
 and piers,
But a home is built of loving deeds that stand a thousand
 years:
A house, though but an humble cot, within its walls may
 hold
A home of priceless beauty, rich in love's eternal gold.

The men of earth build houses,—halls and chambers, roofs
 and domes,—
But the women of the earth,—God knows!—the women
 build the homes;
Eve could not stray from Paradise, for, oh, no matter
 where
Her gracious presence lit the way, lo! Paradise was there.

NIXON WATERMAN

THE BIXBY LETTER

Washington
November 21, 1864

DEAR MADAM:

I have been shown in the file of
the War Department a statement of the
Adjutant General of Massachusetts, that you
are the mother of five sons who have died
gloriously on the field of battle. I feel
how weak and fruitless must be any word of
mine which should attempt to beguile you
from the grief of a loss so overwhelming;
but I cannot refrain from tendering to you
the consolation that may be found in the
thanks of the republic they died to save.
I pray that our heavenly Father may assuage
the anguish of your bereavements, and leave
only the cherished memory of the loved and
lost, and the solemn pride that must be yours
to have laid so costly a sacrifice upon the
altar of freedom.

Yours, very sincerely and respectfully,

A. LINCOLN

"ALL that I am or ever hope to be, I
owe to my sainted Mother."

ABRAHAM LINCOLN

GROWING OLD

At six I well remember when
I fancied all folks old at ten.

But when I turned my first decade,
Fifteen appeared more truly staid.

But when the fifteenth round I'd run,
I thought none old 'til twenty-one.

Then, oddly, when I'd reached that age,
I held that thirty made folks sage.

But when my thirtieth year was told
I said, "At two score men grow old!"

Yet two score came and found me thrifty,
And so I drew the line at fifty.

But when I reached that age, I swore,
None could be old until three score.

And here I am at seventy now,
As young as when at seven, I trow!

'Tis true my hair is somewhat gray,
And that I use a cane today;

'Tis true these rogues about my knee,
Say "Grandpa," when they speak to me;

But, bless your soul, I'm young as when
I thought all people old at ten!

Perhaps a little wiser grown—
Perhaps some old illusions flown;

But wondering still, while years have tolled,
When it is that a man grows old.

MARC EUGENE COOK

THE FLAG GOES BY

HATS off!
Along the street there comes
A blare of bugles, a ruffle of drums,
A flash of color beneath the sky:
Hats off!
The flag is passing by!

Blue and crimson and white it shines,
Over the steel-tipped, ordered lines.
Hats off!
The colors before us fly;
But more than the flag is passing by:

Sea-fights and land-fights, grim and great,
Fought to make and to save the State;
Weary marches and sinking ships;
Cheers of victory on dying lips;

Days of plenty and years of peace;
March of a strong land's swift increase;
Equal justice, right and law,
Stately honor and reverend awe;

Sign of a nation, great and strong
To ward her people from foreign wrong;
Pride and glory and honor,—all
Live in the colors to stand or fall.

Hats off!
Along the street there comes
A blare of bugles, a ruffle of drums;
And loyal hearts are beating high:
Hats off!
The flag is passing by!
HENRY HOLCOMB BENNETT

A WAY TO A HAPPY NEW YEAR

TO LEAVE the old with a burst of song,
To recall the right and forgive the wrong;
To forget the thing that binds you fast
To the vain regrets of the year that's past;
To have the strength to let go your hold
Of the not-worth-while of the days grown old;
To dare go forth with a purpose true
To the unknown task of the world that's new;
To help your brother along the road
To do his work and to lift his load;
To add your gift to the world's good cheer,
Is to have and to give a Happy New Year.
ROBERT BREWSTER BEATTIE

WASHINGTON

ON THAT name no eulogy is
expected. It cannot be.

To add brightness to the sun,—
or glory to the name of Washington, is
alike impossible. Let no one attempt it.

In solemn awe we pronounce the
name, and in its naked, deathless splendor,
leave it to shine on.

ABRAHAM LINCOLN

STANZA

(From Maidenhood)

LIKE the swell of some sweet tune,
Morning rises into noon,
May glides onward into June.

HENRY WADSWORTH LONGFELLOW

HIS TAPESTRY AND MINE

I WEAVE upon my tapestry,
With colors dark and fair;
Some represent a lovely dream,
Some colors are a prayer!
Some colors stand for lonely days,
Some stand for happiness,
Some are as somber as a storm,
Some soft as a caress.

I weave upon my tapestry,
I make a brave design
And what I like about it best,
Is that it's wholly mine!
And yet it is not mine alone,
Ah, that I understand!
For as I weave my tapestry,
God's fingers guide my hand.
                    MARGARET E. SANGSTER

AN APRIL SONG

Now, once more, the crocus flames,
　The tulip lifts its cup;
And over every green morass,
Beyond the utmost lengths of grass,
　Earth drinks the wonder up.

There is a glory in the world;
　The morning is like wine,
And pale ascension lilies lean
Like gods who late in heaven have been,
　Half flowerlike, half divine.

O sweet revival of the grass!
　O sweeter songs that rise,
When jocund April leads her train
Through the gold sunlight and the rain,
　And earth is paradise.

CHARLES HANSON TOWNE

OVERHEARD IN AN ORCHARD

SAID the robin to the sparrow,
"I should really like to know
Why these anxious human beings
Rush about and worry so."

Said the sparrow to the robin,
"Friend, I think that it must be
That they have no Heavenly Father
Such as cares for you and me."
                    ELIZABETH CHENEY

A DREAM OF SPRING

(*From Work Without Hope*)

ALL nature seems at work. Slugs leave their lair,—
The bees are stirring,—birds are on the wing,—
And Winter, slumbering in the open air,
Wears on his smiling face a dream of Spring!
                    SAMUEL TAYLOR COLERIDGE

GOD'S GARDEN

THE Lord God planted a garden
   In the first white days of the world,
And set there an angel warden,
   In a garment of light enfurled.

So near to the peace of Heaven,
   The hawk might nest with the wren;
For there, in the cool of the even,
   God walked with the first of men.

And I dream that these garden closes,
   With their shade and their sun-flecked sod,
And their lilies and bowers of roses,
   Were laid by the hand of God.

The kiss of the sun for pardon,
   The song of the birds for mirth—
One is nearer God's heart in a garden
   Than anywhere else on earth.
                DOROTHY FRANCES GURNEY

YOU HAVE TO BELIEVE

You have to believe in happiness,
　Or happiness never comes.
I know that a bird chirps none the less
　When all that he finds is crumbs.
You have to believe the buds will blow,—
Believe in the grass in the days of snow;
　Ah, that's the reason a bird can sing—
On his darkest day he believes in Spring.

You have to believe in happiness—
　It isn't an outward thing.
The Spring never makes the song, I guess,
　As much as the song the Spring.
Aye, many a heart could find content
If it saw the joy on the road it went,
　The joy ahead when it had to grieve,
For the joy is there—but you have to believe.

Douglas Malloch

GOD'S IN HIS HEAVEN

(From Pippa Passes)

THE year's at the spring
And day's at the morn;
Morning's at seven;
The hillside's dew-pearled;
The lark's on the wing;
The snail's on the thorn:
God's in His heaven—
All's right with the world!
ROBERT BROWNING

THE DOOR IS OPEN

MY DOOR is on the latch tonight,
The hearth fire is aglow,
I seem to hear swift passing feet,
The Christ Child in the snow.

My heart is open wide tonight
For stranger, kith or kin
I would not bar a single door
Where Love might enter in.
KATE DOUGLAS WIGGIN

TO THE FRINGED GENTIAN

Thou blossom bright with autumn dew,
And colored with the heaven's own blue,
That openest when the quiet light
Succeeds the keen and frosty night.

Thou comest not when violets lean
O'er wandering brooks and springs unseen,
Or columbines, in purple dressed,
Nod o'er the ground-bird's hidden nest.

Thou waitest late and com'st alone,
When woods are bare and birds are flown,
And frost and shortening days portend
The aged year is near his end.

Then doth thy sweet and quiet eye
Look through its fringes to the sky,
Blue—blue—as if that sky let fall
A flower from its cerulean wall.

I would that thus, when I shall see
The hour of death draw near to me,
Hope, blossoming within my heart,
May look to heaven as I depart.

WILLIAM CULLEN BRYANT

THE WONDERFUL WORLD

GREAT, wide, beautiful, wonderful World,
With the wonderful water round you curled,
And the wonderful grass upon your breast,
World, you are beautifully dressed.

The wonderful air is over me,
And the wonderful wind is shaking the tree—
It walks on the water, and whirls the mills,
And talks to itself on the tops of the hills.

You friendly Earth, how far do you go,
With the wheat-fields that nod and the rivers that flow,
With cities and gardens, and cliffs and isles,
And people upon you for thousands of miles?

Ah! you are so great, and I am so small,
I tremble to think of you, World, at all;
And yet, when I said my prayers today,
A whisper inside me seemed to say,
"You are more than the Earth, though you are such a dot:
You can love and think, and the Earth cannot!"

WILLIAM BRIGHTY RANDS

TREES

I THINK that I shall never see
A poem lovely as a tree.

A tree whose hungry mouth is prest
Against the earth's sweet flowing breast;

A tree that looks at God all day,
And lifts her leafy arms to pray;

A tree that may in Summer wear
A nest of robins in her hair;

Upon whose bosom snow has lain;
Who intimately lives with rain.

Poems are made by fools like me,
But only God can make a tree.

JOYCE KILMER

TRIBUTE

THIS angel's prayer is very small,
(For angels seldom pray at all!)
She asks—"Through tempests, frosts and snows,
Take care, dear God, of Major Bowes!"

MARGARET E. SANGSTER

JUNE FOURTEENTH

(Birthday Tribute to Major Bowes by his sister)

ONCE upon a summer's day,
A little boy did find his way,
Into this world of joy and strife,
And so began his little life.

Upon a ladder he did put,
A weak and tender little foot;
But gazing upward he did smile,
And thought "It may take me a while,
But someday I shall top that pile."

So, step by step, and rung by rung,
The boy, although so very young,
Went on and up, and every year,
E'en though his climb oft cost a tear,
There burned within a constant fire,
That never let him flag nor tire.

So, on and up, a steady climb;
It mattered not that many a time,
There loomed ahead an ominous cloud;
His spirit, always firm and proud,
Refused to slacken or to pall,
For from within he heard the call
To forge ahead and never fall.

And so the years sped quickly by,
With many a laugh and many a sigh;
Teaching lessons, bitter, sweet,
Giving a blow, and then a treat;
Breaking down a fond illusion,
Clearing up a sad confusion,
Offering strength to a steadfast soul,
To one who forges ahead to his goal.

And now, through sunshine and dark of night,
The top of the ladder is well in sight.
And there is much to greet the eye,
To make one glad, to make one cry.
The joys and griefs of yesteryear
Are far away and yet so near;
For memories follow in our wake,
To give us joy, yet joy to take,
Our hearts to cheer, our hearts to break.

Again it is a summer's day;
The little boy has had his way.
He gazes down the row of years,
He smiles content, e'en through his tears,
With all the pride of well earned fame,
He knows success is just a name,
Unless somewhere in this sad vale,
There lives one heart that cannot fail.
Alas, we mortals have such need,
For love alone the soul can feed.

L'envoi
Oh, come again, bright summer's day;
Come, and well your homage pay.
Each year return, and bring pure joy
To him who was that little boy.
CAROLINE BOWES TOMBO

THE DAY IS DONE

THE day is done, and the darkness
Falls from the wings of Night,
As a feather is wafted downward
From an eagle in his flight. . . .

And the night shall be filled with music,
And the cares, that infest the day,
Shall fold their tents, like the Arabs,
And as silently steal away.
HENRY WADSWORTH LONGFELLOW

A JOURNEY

LIFE is like a journey
  Taken on a train
With a pair of travelers
  At each window pane.
I may sit beside you
  All the journey through,
Or I may sit elsewhere
  Never knowing you.
But if fate should mark me
  To sit by your side,
Let's be pleasant travelers;
  It's so short a ride.
DR. M. COLEMAN HARRIS

GARDENING

To DIG and delve in nice clean dirt
Can do a mortal little hurt;
Who works with roses soon will find
Their fragrance budding in his mind,
And minds that sprout with roses free,—
Well, that's the sort of mind for me!
JOHN KENDRICK BANGS

POEMS BY UNKNOWN AUTHORS

It makes no difference who sang the song,
If only the song was sung;
It makes no difference who did the deed,
Be they old in years or young;
If the song was sweet and helped a soul,
What matters the singer's name?
The worth was in the song itself,
And not in the world's acclaim.
The song and the deed are one
If each be done for love;
Love of the work, not love of self,
And the "score" is kept above.

THE BLIND WEAVER

A BLIND boy stood beside the loom
And wove a fabric. To and fro
Beneath his firm and steady touch
He made the busy shuttle go.

And oft the teacher passed that way
And gave the colors, thread by thread;
But to the boy the pattern fair
Was all unseen—its hues were dead.

"How can you weave?" we, pitying, cried;
The blind boy smiled, "I do my best;
I make the fabric firm and strong,
And one who sees does all the rest."

Oh, happy thought! Beside Life's loom
We blindly strive our best to do,
And He who marked the pattern out,
And holds the threads, will make it true.

LUCK

THE "luck" that I believe in
Is that which comes with work;
But no one ever finds it
Who's content to wish and shirk;
The men the world call "lucky"
Will tell you, every one,
Success comes not with wishing,
But by hard work, bravely done.

A WISH

MAY you live a thousand years
And I a thousand less one day
So that I may never know you passed away.

A LITTLE SEED OF LOVE

If I can plant some little seed of love
That later on will blossom in a smile,
It matters not however else I fail;
My life will be worth-while.

If I can do some little kindly act
That later on may soothe some sad heart's pain,
It matters not what else I do, my life
Will not have been in vain.

LIVE AND LOVE

Why does the road wind ever away
Till we cannot see the end?
Why do we climb and climb each day?
Where does it lead, good friend?
Where does it lead but up and away?
Why need we see the end,
If we work and sing and climb each day
And live and love, good friend?

THIS LIFE IS WHAT WE MAKE IT

LET's oftener talk of noble deeds,
　　And rarer of the bad ones,
And sing about our happy days,
　　And not about the sad ones,
We were not made to fret and sigh,
　　And when grief sleeps to wake it,
Bright happiness is standing by—
　　This life is what we make it.

Let's find the sunny side of men,
　　Or be believers in it:
A light there is in every soul
　　That takes the pains to win it.
O! there's a slumbering good in all,
　　And we perchance may wake it;
Our hands contain the magic wand:
　　This life is what we make it.

Then here's to those whose loving hearts
　　Shed light and joy about them!
Thanks be to them for countless gems
　　We ne'er had known without them.
O! this should be a happy world
　　To all who may partake it;
The fault's our own if it is not—
　　This life is what we make it.

IT'S ALL IN THE STATE OF MIND

IF YOU think you are beaten, you are,
   If you think that you dare not, you don't,
If you'd like to win, but you think you can't,
   It's almost certain you won't.
If you think you'll lose, you've lost,
   For out in the world you'll find
Success begins with a fellow's will—
   It's all in the state of mind.

Full many a race is lost
   Ere even a step is run,
And many a coward falls
   Ere even his work's begun.
Think big, and your deeds will grow;
   Think small, and you'll fall behind;
Think that you can, and you will—
   It's all in the state of mind.

If you think you are out-classed, you are;
   You've got to think high to rise;
You've got to be sure of yourself before
   You can ever win a prize.
Life's battles don't always go
   To the stronger or faster man;
But soon or late the man who wins
   Is the man who thinks he can.

SUCCESS

BEFORE God's footstool to confess
A poor soul knelt, and bowed his head;
"I failed," he cried. The Master said
"Thou didst thy best—that is success!"

CONTENT

A HERMIT there was
    Who lived in a grot,
And the way to be happy
    They said he had got.
As I wanted to learn it,
    I went to his cell;
And this answer he gave,
    As I asked him to tell:

" 'Tis *being*, and *doing*,
    And *having* that make
All the pleasures and pains
    Of which mortals partake.
To *be* what God pleases,
    To *do* what is best,
And to *have* a good heart
    Is the way to be blest."

A PRAYER FOUND IN CHESTER CATHEDRAL

Give me a good digestion, Lord,
And also something to digest;
Give me a healthy body, Lord,
With sense to keep it at its best.

Give me a healthy mind, good Lord,
To keep the good and pure in sight;
Which, seeing sin, is not appalled,
But finds a way to set it right.

Give me a mind that is not bored,
That does not whimper, whine or sigh;
Don't let me worry overmuch,
About the fussy thing called "I."

Give me a sense of humor, Lord;
Give me the grace to see a joke;
To get some happiness from life,
And pass it on to other folk.

LIVE IN THE PRESENT

WOULD you keep young and happy and strong?
Then think not of the past,
Nor of the things that may belong
Unto the future vast.
Live in the present, and you will find
A joy that's sweet, and peace of mind.

BE CHEERFUL

BE CHEERFUL! Give this lonesome world a smile;
We stay, at longest, but a little while.
Hasten we must, or we shall lose the chance
To give the gentle word, the kindly glance.
Be sweet and tender: that is doing good;
'Tis doing what no other good deed could.

TELL HIM SO

IF YOU hear a kind word spoken
  Of some worthy soul you know,
It may fill his heart with sunshine
  If you only tell him so.

If a deed, however humble,
  Helps you on your way to go,
Seek the one whose hand has helped you,
  Seek him out and tell him so.

If your heart is touched and tender
  Towards a sinner, lost and low;
It might help him to do better
  If you'd only tell him so.

WAKE UP TOMORROW MORNING

WAKE up tomorrow morning
A new word in your mind;
Wake up tomorrow morning
Determined to be kind.
A little smile of greeting,
Some friendly word you say,
Will make the man you're meeting
Feel better all the day.

[133]

DO SOMETHING

Do SOMETHING for somebody somewhere,
　　While jogging along life's road;
Help someone to carry his burden,
　　And lighter will grow your load.

Do something for somebody, gladly,
　　'Twill sweeten your every care;
In sharing the sorrows of others
　　Your own are less hard to bear.

Do something for somebody, striving
　　To help where the way seems long;
And the sorrowful hearts that languish
　　Cheer up with a little song.

Do something for somebody always,
　　Whatever may be your creed—
There's nothing on earth can help you
　　So much as a kindly deed.

MR. MEANT-TO

MR. MEANT-TO has a comrade,
And his name is Didn't-Do.
Have you ever chanced to meet them?
Did they ever call on you?

These two fellows live together
In the House of Never-Win
And I'm told that it is haunted
By the ghost of Might-Have-Been.

A LITTLE RHYME

GIVE a little, live a little, try a little mirth;
Sing a little, bring a little happiness to earth;
Pray a little, play a little, be a little glad;
Rest a little, jest a little, if the heart is sad.
Spend a little, send a little to another's door;
Give a little, live a little, love a little more.

I WONDER

AN OLD man limped along life's way
His grief-bowed head was crowned with grey;
Somebody cheered his dreary day;
            I wonder—was it you?

There's always someone needing aid,
Some trembling heart alone, afraid;
Some load that could be lighter made—
            Can they depend on you?

A SMILE

A SMILE is like a little wedge
That often keeps us from the edge
Of getting sad, or feeling blue—
I love to see a smile, don't you?

LOVING WORDS

LOVING words will cost but little,
　　Journeying up the hill of life;
But they make the weak and weary
　　Stronger, braver, for the strife.
Do you count them only trifles?
　　What to earth are sun and rain?
Never was a kind word wasted,
　　Never one was said in vain.

When the cares of life are many,
　　And its burdens heavy grow,
Think of weak ones close beside you—
　　If you love them, tell them so.
What you count of little value
　　Has an almost magic power,
And beneath their cheering sunshine
　　Hearts will blossom like a flower.

So, as up life's hill we journey,
　　Let us scatter all the way
Kindly words, for they are sunshine
　　In the dark and cloudy day.
Grudge no loving word or action
　　As along through life you go,
There are weary ones around you—
　　If you love them, tell them so.

THE DOLLAR AND THE CENT

A big silver dollar and a little brown cent—
　Rolling along together they went,
Rolling along the smooth sidewalk,
　When the dollar remarked—for the dollar can talk,
You poor little cent, you cheap little mite,
　I'm bigger and more than twice as bright;
I'm worth more than you a hundredfold,
　And written on me in letters bold
Is the motto drawn from the pious creed,
　"In God We Trust," which all can read.
I know, said the cent, I'm a cheap little mite,
　And I know I'm not big, nor good, nor bright.
And yet, said the cent, with a meek little sigh,
　You don't go to Church as often as I.

THE WAY TO HAPPINESS

KEEP your heart free from hate, your mind from worry.
Live simply; expect little; give much; fill your life with
love; scatter sunshine. Forget self. Think of others, and
do as you would be done by.

MINUTES OF GOLD

Two or three minutes—two or three hours,
What do they mean in this life of ours?
Not very much if but counted as time,
But minutes of gold and hours sublime,
If only we'll use them once in a while
To make someone happy—make someone smile.
A minute may dry a little lad's tears,
An hour sweep aside trouble of years.
Minutes of my time may bring to an end,
Hopelessness somewhere, and bring me a friend.

LOOKING AND OVERLOOKING

If we noticed little pleasures
    As we notice little pains;
If we quite forgot our losses
    And remembered all our gains;
If we looked for people's virtues,
    And their faults refused to see;
What a comfortable, happy,
    Cheerful place this world would be!

[139]

GROWING SMILES

A SMILE is quite a funny thing,
It wrinkles up your face,
And when it's gone, you never find
Its secret hiding place.

But far more wonderful it is
To see what smiles can do;
You smile at one, he smiles at you,
And so one smile makes two.

He smiles at someone since you smiled,
And then that one smiles back;
And that one smiles, until in truth
You fail in keeping track.

Now since a smile can do great good
By cheering hearts of care,
Let's smile and smile, and not forget
That smiles go everywhere!

OLD PROVERB

For every evil under the sun
There is a remedy, or there's none;
If there is one, try and find it;
If there is none, never mind it.

FACE THE SUN

Don't hunt for trouble, but look for success;
You'll find what you look for—don't look for distress.
If you see but your shadow, remember I pray
That the sun is still shining, but you're in the way.

Don't grumble, don't bluster, don't dream and don't
    shirk;
Don't think of your worries, but think of your work.
The worries will vanish, the work will be done,
No man sees his shadow, who faces the sun.

DON'T QUIT

WHEN things go wrong, as they sometimes will,
When the road you're trudging seems all uphill,
When the funds are low and the debts are high
And you want to smile, but you have to sigh,
When care is pressing you down a bit,
Rest! if you must—but never quit.

Life is queer, with its twists and turns,
As every one of us sometimes learns,
And many a failure turns about
When he might have won if he'd stuck it out.
Stick to your task, though the pace seems slow,
You may succeed with another blow.

Often the goal is nearer than
It seems to a faint and faltering man.
Often the struggler has given up
When he might have captured the victor's cup,
And he learned too late, when the night slipped down,
How close he was to the golden crown.

Success is failure turned inside out,
The silver tints of the clouds of doubt,
And you never can tell how close you are,—
It may be near when it seems afar.
So stick to the fight when you're hardest hit,—
It's when things seem worst that you mustn't quit.

IT CAN'T BE DONE

THE man who misses all the fun
Is he who says, "It can't be done."
In solemn pride he stands aloof
And greets each venture with reproof.
Had he the power he'd efface
The history of the human race;
We'd have no radio or trolley cars,
No streets lit by electric stars;
No telegraph nor telephone,
We'd linger in the age of stone.
The world would sleep if things were run
By men who say "It can't be done."

BEST WISHES

MAY the sun be warm and kind to you;
The darkest night some star shine through;
The dullest morn a radiance bloom,
And when dusk comes—God's hand to you!

[143]

DO IT NOW

IF YOU have hard work to do,
    Do it now.
Today the skies are clear and blue,
Tomorrow clouds may come in view,
Yesterday is not for you;
    Do it now.

If you have a song to sing,
    Sing it now.
Let the tones of gladness ring
Clear as song of bird in spring.
Let each day some music bring;
    Sing it now.

If you have kind words to say,
    Say them now.
Tomorrow may not come your way,
Do a kindness while you may,
Loved ones will not always stay;
    Say them now.

If you have a smile to show,
    Show it now.
Make hearts happy, roses grow,
Let the friends around you know
The love you have before they go;
    Show it now.

COURAGE

COURAGE for the great sorrows of life, and patience for the small ones; and then when you have accomplished your daily task, go to sleep in peace. God is awake.

ONLY A LITTLE

JUST a little smile will cheer us
When life's hill is very steep;
Just a kindly word will help us
When a frown would make us weep.
Just the sunshine on the waters,
Just the rainbow in the sky,
Just a little love, so little,
And its value is so high.

THE GLAD GAME

LET's play we are glad, it's a thrilling game,
    And the playing will be sweet;
Let's say we are glad, say it joyfully
    Every time we meet.

Let's play we are glad and say we are glad,
    (It need not, of course, be true)
But I'll venture to say we will be glad
    Before the game is through.

A MIRROR

THE world is like a mirror,
    Reflecting what you do,
And if your face is smiling
    It smiles right back at you.

SING YOU A SONG

SING you a song in the garden of life,
    If only you gather a thistle;
Sing you a song as you travel along,
    And if you can't sing, why just whistle!

IS IT WISDOM TO WORRY?

WHEN things go contrary as often they do,
And fortune seems burdened with spite,
Don't give way to grieving dismal and blue;
That never sets anything right.
Cheerfully face what the day will reveal
Make the best of whate'er may befall,
Since the more you worry the worse you feel,
Is it wisdom to worry at all?

KEEP A–SMILIN'

It's good to keep a-smilin',
For a smile's a kind of net,
That catches by beguilin'
Just the things it wants to get.
So keep your smile a-spreadin',
Crack a jolly joke or two,
And you'll find that things
Come headin' straight
For smilin' folks like you.

WORRIES—AT EIGHTY

He was eighty years of age that day;
He had lived the allotted span;
He had carried burdens hard to bear;
He was every inch a man;
'Twas on this birthday that he said
Of worries great and small:
"The things that never happened
Were the biggest of them all."

TROUBLES

I **WROTE** down my troubles every day,
And after a few short years,
When I thought of the heartaches passed away,
I read them with smiles, not tears.

A SONG

IF YOU frown at life
  As you go your way,
And grumble and growl
  The livelong day,
You'll find the world
  Is a sorry place,
A gloomy affair,
  Like your frowning face.

But sing a song,
  Like a playful lad,
And whistle a tune,
  Like a youngster glad;
You'll find the world
  Will smile at you,
The sun will shine,
  And the skies be blue.

HOLD UP YOUR CHIN

PLUCK brings its reward,
Reverses don't kill,
If fate hits you hard
Strike back with a will.
Let it do what it can,
Still hold up your chin
For the world loves a man
Who never gives in.

THE CHARM OF SWEET CONTENTMENT

THE best things are the simplest things—home and love
and work to do, flowers in the garden, and bread from
the generous fields.

Lacking these, what else can make life worth the living?
Having them, give thanks with joy; we need no more.

THE LOOM OF TIME

MAN's life is laid in the loom of time
    To a pattern he does not see,
While the weavers work and the shuttles fly
    Till the dawn of eternity.

Some shuttles are filled with silver threads
    And some with threads of gold,
While often but the darker hues
    Are all that they may hold.

But the weaver watches with skillful eye
    Each shuttle fly to and fro,
And sees the pattern so deftly wrought
    As the loom moves sure and slow.

God surely planned the pattern,
    Each thread, the dark and fair,
Is chosen by His master skill
    And placed in the web with care.

He only knows its beauty,
    And guides the shuttles which hold
The threads so unattractive,
    As well as the threads of gold.

Not till each loom is silent
    And the shuttles cease to fly,
Shall God reveal the pattern
    And explain the reason why

The dark threads were as needful
In the weaver's skillful hand
As the threads of gold and silver
For the pattern which He planned.

OUR CHRISTMAS PRESENTS

WHEN we give to each other our Christmas presents, let us give them in His name.

Let us remember that He has given us the sun and the moon and the stars, the earth with its forests and mountains and oceans and all that lives and moves upon them.

He has given us all green things and everything that blossoms and bears fruit—and all that we quarrel about and all that we have misused.

And to save us from our own foolishness and from all our sins, He came down to Earth and gave Himself.

THE WORRY OF IT

IT IS not the work but the worry
   That makes the world grow old;
That numbers the years of its children
   Ere half their story is told;
That weakens their faith in heaven
   And the wisdom of God's great plan.
Ah! 'tis not the work but the worry
   That breaks the heart of man!

RISE A LITTLE HIGHER

THOSE who live on the mountain have a longer day than those who live in the valley. Sometimes all we need to brighten our day is to rise a little higher.

OPINION

WHAT one approves, another scorns,
And thus his nature each discloses:
You find the rosebush full of thorns,
I find the thornbush full of roses.

FRIENDSHIP

FRIENDSHIP needs no symbol,
Or vow to make it whole;
It's just a sacred covenant
That's locked within the soul;
It knows no creed or station,
Or thought of gain or fame,
For what it does is sacred,
And is done in Friendship's name.

HOW OLD ARE YOU?

AGE is a quality of mind.
If you have left your dreams behind,
If hope is cold,
If you no longer look ahead,
If your ambitions' fires are dead—
Then you are old.

But if from life you take the best,
And if in life you keep the jest,
If love you hold;
No matter how the years go by,
No matter how the birthdays fly—
You are not old.

REV. H. SAMUEL FRITSCH, D.D.

THE LOOM

THE loom of time has ever been
A pattern weaving, all unseen,
Wise folks teach children soon to see,
And weave their patterns carefully.

[155]

THE SALUTATION OF THE DAWN

LISTEN to the salutation of the dawn!
　Look to this day!
For it is life, the very life of life;
In its brief course lie all the realities
And verities of your existence;
　The bliss of growth,
　The glory of action,
　The splendor of beauty,
For yesterday is but a dream
And to-morrow but a vision;
But to-day well-lived makes every yesterday
　A dream of happiness,
And every to-morrow a vision of hope.
Look well, therefore, to this day!
Such is the salutation of the dawn!
                    FROM THE SANSKRIT

HAPPINESS

WHERE's happiness? That city fair
I sought in vain to find.
A friend located it for me:
It's in the state of mind.

VALENTINE'S DAY

THOUGH you already know it,
I'll tell you one more time
That you are still the only one
Who is my Valentine.
And saying it this minute
Convinces me anew
I was a lucky person
The day that I met you.

GIVE ME A FRIEND

GIVE me a friend and I'll worry along:
My vision may vanish, my dream may go wrong;
My wealth I may lose, or my money may spend;
But I'll worry along, if you give me a friend.

Give me a friend, and my youth may depart
But still I'll be young in the house of my heart,
Yes, I'll go laughing right on to the end
Whatever the years, if you give me a friend.

[157]

I WEAVE FOR THEE

By NIGHT and day I weave for thee,
A golden, gleaming net of prayer,
Its shining mesh thou mayest not see,
But it surrounds thee everywhere.
God bless thy peaceful sleep by night,
God bless thy busy steps by day,
Keep faith within thy heart alight,
In clouds or sunshine—this I pray.

THE FINEST THINGS

The finest things in life are those
    We neither sell nor buy;
A bursting bud—a bird that sings,
    A glowing western sky.
And friends to love—these are indeed
    Well worth their weight in gold—
And may you know the gladness which
    Such things forever hold.

[158]

THE BLESSED NAME OF MOTHER

THE noblest thoughts my soul can claim,
The holiest words my tongue can frame,
Unworthy are to praise the name,
More sacred than all other.

An infant when her love first came;
A man, I find it just the same;
Reverently I breathe her name—
The blessed name of "Mother."

MOTHER LOVE

A MOTHER'S smile,—a Mother's kiss,
Your life can hold no greater bliss.
Each thought a hope, each word a prayer,
She holds you in her loving care.
God sent His spirit from above
And formed it into Mother-love.

BENEDICTION

BLESSED are they who are pleasant to live with,
Blessed are they who sing in the morning,
Whose faces have smiles for this early adorning;
Who come down to breakfast companioned by cheer,
Who won't dwell on trouble, nor entertain fear,
Whose eyes shine forth bravely, whose lips curve to say,
Life, I salute you, good morrow, new day.

Blessed are they who are pleasant to live with,
Blessed are they who treat one another,
Though merely a sister, a father, a brother
With the very same courtesy they would extend
To a casual acquaintance, or dearly loved friend;
Who choose for the telling encouraging things,
And choke back the bitter, the sharp word that stings.

Blessed are they who are pleasant to live with,
Blessed are they who give of their best,
Who bring to the home bright laughter, gay jest,
Who make themselves charming for no other reason,
Than charm is a blossom for home every season;
Who bestow love on others throughout the long day,
Pleasant to live with, and blessed are they.

THROUGH THE DISTANCE AND THE DARK

How many million friends there are whose lot
Keeps them outside my path for life's short while!
But through the distance and the dark I smile
For I can love them,—though I see them not.

TO ALL FRIENDS

LOVE is not stuff to gather dust on shelves!
The more we give, the more we have ourselves;
So all our love we send to you, and then
Yet more we'll have to send to you again.

ARTHUR GUITERMAN

POLITENESS

TO BE polite is to do and say
The kindest things in the kindest way.

A FAME THAT NEVER ENDS

(In Memory of William H. Woodin)

HE WAS a friend
    Whose heart was good;
Who walked with men
    And understood;
His was a voice
    That spoke to cheer,
And fell like music
    On the ear.
His was a smile
    Men loved to see;
His was a hand
    That asked no fee
For friendliness
    Or kindness done.
And now that he
    Has journeyed on,
His is a fame
    That never ends;
He leaves behind
    Uncounted friends.

'TIS A LITTLE JOURNEY

'Tis a little journey
    This we walk;
Hardly time for murmurs—
    Time for talk.

Yet we learn to quarrel
    And to hate;
'Afterwards regret it
    When too late.

Now and then 'tis sunshine—
    Sometimes dark;
Sometimes care and sorrow
    Leave their mark.

Yet we walk the pathway
    Side by side;
Where so many others
    Lived and died.

We can see the moral,
    Understand;
Yet we walk not always
    Hand in hand.

Why must there be hatred?
    Greed and strife?
Do we need such shadows
    Here in life?

'Tis a little journey
    Soon gone by;
Let's be friends together
    Ere we die!

[163]

MAKING A GARDEN

MAN plows and plants and digs and weeds
    He works with hoe and spade;
God sends the sun and rain and air
    And thus a garden's made.

He must be proud who tills the soil
    And turns the heavy sod,
How wonderful a thing to be
    In partnership with God!

GOD GIVE ME STRENGTH

EACH day I pray, God give me strength anew
To do the task I do not wish to do;
To yield obedience, not asking why;
To love and own the truth, and scorn the lie;
To look a cold world in the face;
To cheer for those who pass me in the race;
To bear my burdens gaily, unafraid;
To lend a hand to those who need my aid;
To measure what I am, by what I give—
God give me strength that I may rightly live!

FRIENDS OLD AND NEW

MAKE new friends, but keep the old,—
Those are silver, these are gold;
New-made friendships, like new wine,
Age will mellow and refine.

Friendships that have stood the test—
Time and change—are surely best;
Brow may wrinkle, hair grow gray,
Friendship never knows decay.

For 'mid old friends, tried and true,
Once more we our youth renew;
But old friends, alas, may die,
New friends must their place supply.

Cherish Friendship in your breast;
New is good, but old is best;
Make new friends, but keep the old,—
Those are silver, these are gold.

FIVE THINGS TO OBSERVE

IF YOU your lips would keep from slips,
   Five things observe with care—
To whom you speak, of whom you speak,
   And how, and when and where.

If you your ears would keep from jeers,
   These things keep meekly hid—
Myself and me, or my and mine,
   And how I do or did.

STOP AND THINK

IT's a little thing to do—
   Just to think;
Anyone, no matter who,
   Ought to think.
Take a little time each day
From the minutes thrown away;
Spare it from your work or play;
   Stop and *think*.

THE MEASURE OF A MAN

Not—"How did he die?" But—"How did he live?"
Not—"What did he gain?" But—"What did he give?"
 These are the units to measure the worth
 Of a man as a man, regardless of birth.

Not—"What was his station?" But—"Had he a heart?"
And—"How did he play his God-given part?
 Was he ever ready with a word of good cheer,
 To bring back a smile, to banish a tear?"

Not—"What was his church?" Nor—"What was his
 creed?"
But—"Had he befriended those really in need?"
Not—"What did the sketch in the newspaper say?"
But—"How many were sorry when he passed away?"

A GOLDEN CLOCK

(*In Memory of Holbrook Blinn*)

Since you are gone so far away
 A curious thing I find;
The world is like a golden clock
 That God forgot to wind.

[167]

GOD BLESS YOU

I SEEK in prayerful words, dear friend,
My heart's true wish to send you,
That you may know that, far or near,
My loving thoughts attend you.

I cannot find a truer word,
Nor better to address you;
Nor song, nor poem have I heard
Is sweeter than God bless you!

God bless you! So I've wished you all
Of brightness life possesses;
For can there any joy at all
Be yours unless God blesses?

God bless you! so I breathe a charm
Lest grief's dark night oppress you,
For how can sorrow bring you harm
If 'tis God's way to bless you.

And so, "through all thy days
May shadows touch thee never—"
But this alone—God bless thee—
Then art thou safe forever.

A BLESSING

GIVE this house, O traveler, pray,
A blessing as you pass this way.
And if you've time, I beg your pardon,
While you're at it—bless the garden.

RECIPE

TAKE one large, grassy field,
One-half dozen children,
Two or three small dogs,
A pinch of brook and some pebbles.
Mix the children and the dogs well together
And put them in the field constantly stirring;
Pour the brook over the pebbles;
Sprinkle the field with flowers;
Spread over all a deep blue sky
And bake in the hot sun.
When brown, remove and set away to cool—in a bathtub!

AT CYPRESS LAWN

'Tis sweet to believe in a Heaven
As being a beautiful shore
Where long-sundered hearts are united
To part from each other no more.
And this is what lightens my burden
Since death rent our bosoms in twain,
That there, in that ultimate harbor,
Our love will burn brightly again.

OUR JUDGE

Unthanked, unnoticed and unknown,
Blamed sometimes and misunderstood;
Yet if our Lord but sees our work,
And by His grace shall own it good,
It will not matter what men say,
Since God is Judge of all, not they.

THE UNDERSTANDING HEART

IN MY intense desire for sight,
May I not stand in someone's light.
And if my neighbour err, I pray,
Oh, show me, then, my feet of clay.
God grant to me the highest art;
Give me the understanding heart.

WORDS

I LOVE the sound of kindly words—
　I try to make them sing,
And hope I never send one out
　To be a hurtful thing.

NO NEED

WHERE there is Faith,
    There is Love.
Where there is Love,
    There is Peace.
Where there is Peace,
    There is God.
Where there is God,
    There is no need.
TRANSLATED FROM THE GERMAN

GOD IS IN THE GARDEN

THERE is healing in a garden
When one longs for peace and pardon.
Once past the gate, no need to wait,
For God is in the garden.

TREES AND THEIR CLOTHES

WHEN the season of warm weather begins, trees put on clothes.

When the summer heat sets in, they put on the thickest clothes obtainable.

When the season becomes cooler, they begin to remove their clothes.

And when the bitter cold of winter arrives, they take off all their clothes.

SALAAM ALAIKUM

(*Peace Be With You*)

I PRAY the Prayer the Easterns do,
May the peace of Allah abide with you.
Wherever you stay, wherever you go,
May the beautiful palms of Allah grow.
Through days of labor and nights of rest,
May the love of good Allah make you blest.
So I touch my heart as the Easterns do,
May the peace of Allah abide with you.

[173]

REST

ARE you very tired? Rest a little bit.
In some quiet corner, fold your hands and sit.
Do not let the trials that have grieved you all the day
Haunt this quiet corner; drive them all away!
Let your heart grow empty of every thought unkind
That good may hover round you, and joy may fill your
    mind.
Count up all your blessings, I'm sure they are not few,
That the dear Lord daily just bestows on you.
Soon you'll feel so rested, glad you stopped a bit,
In this quiet corner, to fold your hands and sit.

PLANT FLOWERS

PLANT Flowers, that thou may'st perfume have—and to
    give;
Plant Cabbages, that thou may'st eat and live,
For life is complex, and its needs demand
That Flowers and Cabbages go hand in hand.

INDEXES

INDEX OF FIRST LINES

[179]

INDEX OF FIRST LINES

INDEX OF FIRST LINES

INDEX OF FIRST LINES

INDEX OF AUTHORS

INDEX OF AUTHORS

INDEX OF TITLES

INDEX OF TITLES

INDEX OF TITLES

INDEX OF TITLES

...ns of millions of people throughout the world who have had
to flee their homes in search of a safe haven, and the thousands of volunteers
who came from all over the globe to help them —D.K.

To all the moms, especially Sura, Susan, Bobo, Chloma, and Karisa —A.S.

To my kind uncle John Fitzpatrick, age 96, who has spent a lifetime
providing a loving home for many, many homeless cats —S.C.

Acknowledgments

Thank you to Hadi Khatib, for helping us to communicate with Kunkush's
family and share their words and feelings with young readers.

And a special thank-you to Michelle Nhin, Ashley Anderson, Emma and
Simon Issatt, Ignatios and Maria Kazantzoglou, and the global community
that made this reunion possible.

Permission to use the following images in "A Remarkable Journey" is gratefully acknowledged: Spread 1—Photograph of Kunkush (top far right)
courtesy of Jeff Bender. Photograph of Kunkush (far center) courtesy of Amy Shrodes. Spread 2—Photograph of Kunkush in Norway
(far bottom left) and the family with Kunkush's carrier (far bottom right) courtesy of Kunkush's family.
Map of Kunkush's journey Shutterstock © Rainer Lesniewski. All other photographs courtesy of Doug Kuntz.

Visit us on the Web! randomhousekids.com

Educators and librarians, for a variety of teaching tools, visit us at RHTeachersLibrarians.com

Library of Congress Cataloging-in-Publication Data is available upon request.
ISBN 978-1-5247-1547-2 (trade)—ISBN 978-1-5247-1548-9 (lib. bdg.)—
ISBN 978-1-5247-1549-6 (ebook)

MANUFACTURED IN CHINA
10 9 8 7 6 5 4 3 2 1
First Edition

Random House Children's Books supports the
First Amendment and celebrates the right to read.